DUTCH PATCHWORK QUILT
Circa 1800-1825

Made from triangles of chintz and printed cotton, 80½" x 106".
This quilt from 200 years ago was the inspiration for the Elizabeth quilt, opposite and on page 56.
Photograph: Nederlands Openluchtmuseum, Arnhem, Netherlands.

Blended
Wall Quilts

SHARON EVANS YENTER

table of Contents

Introduction

The quilts that I call "blended" are not your mother's quilts or your grandmother's quilts. They go back to your great-great-, or even great-great-great-grandmother and the time around 1800 until 1840.

This was an era when precious pieces of fabric were collected and saved in the important family scrap basket. When the original purpose of the cloth was served, it was not discarded but carefully preserved. Fabrics could cover a fifty-year period as quilters waited for the chintz draperies or bed curtains to wear out. This was not a time of planned obsolescence, for these fabrics were sometimes meant to last a lifetime. Because of the period covered, many of the blended quilts were made in the eastern and southern United States, England, Canada, and Holland. The quilts were truly scrap quilts, but elegant scrap quilts!

Many of the luxurious quilts were taken from the East Coast and brought West to become a treasured "best" quilt. The West of the early 1800s was considered Illinois, Minnesota, Nebraska, and surrounding states. It would be many years before the homesteaders in wagon trains would venture toward the Oregon Territory, now known as the Pacific Northwest, where I make my home.

Perhaps that is why I have a fascination with the beautiful "best" quilts. For many years, I only admired them in books because quilts from the early 19th century seldom came this far. About 15 years ago, I visited Great Britain and was lucky enough to find and purchase an English quilt from 1840. I experienced the same feeling I had when I opened my quilt shop — total disbelief and elation that it was actually mine! In the ensuing years I have had the opportunity to see and study early quilts and I continue to be enchanted (en-chant' - to cast a spell over: bewitch, delight greatly). This word defines me when I am near an elegant, rare, and beautiful quilt.

Gorgeous quilts are as fashionable for home decor today as they were 200 years ago. It is not necessary to make quilts as large as those in 1800 (many were 100" x 100") to capture the warmth and sophistication they reflected. Smaller wall quilts can create a welcoming and colorful centerpiece in any room of your home.

The availability of fabrics similar to those of the early 19th century makes it possible to construct quilts reminiscent of that era with your own twist. You can borrow the best of the antique pieces and add a 21st century soul. I hope this technique opens a whole new appreciation of early quiltmaking for you in both a historic and artistic context.

Unit Technique

Getting Started

All eight of the quilts in this workbook were made with simple units that are designed to be interchangeable from one quilt to the next. The finished unit sizes of 1½", 3", 6", and 12" allow all of the pieces to work easily together, and the simplicity of the piecing allows you to concentrate on the really fun part...the fabric! On page 8, you will see how the units can be combined to create easy blocks and borders.

A template method and a quick rotary technique are given so you may choose whichever cutting method you prefer.

Additional blocks are given on page 9 to allow you to design your own wall quilts. These 6" blocks can easily be used in place of any of the 6" blocks in the featured quilt plans (starting on page 40).

Graph paper on pages 10-11 is especially designed to scale: one square = 1½", and allows you to draw your quilt in either a straight or "on point" diagonal set. Copy the page you select on a photocopy machine. Give yourself a good supply of copies so you're prepared whenever inspiration strikes!

Special Notes

Blended quilts make use of large floral fabrics combined with smaller prints, toiles, tonals, stripes, and plaids. To see how these prints work together it is important to create your piece on a vertical surface. Working on a design wall will allow you to view combinations much like a painter sees her canvas.

The quilt patterns list minimal fabric requirements, but you may want to purchase extra fabric, so you can cut additional pieces in more colors and sizes to audition on your design wall. Think of yourself as an artist with a color palette of fabrics to use in exploring your creativity.

Notice that many of the quilts featured include stars in their design. I have found that making star blocks is one of the easiest ways to learn the blended technique. It's hard to go wrong, and is an easy way to practice combining prints and colors without wasting fabric. You can easily insert these blocks into a project and they will look spectacular whether you choose high contrast, low contrast, or no contrast!

Read the Basic Quiltmaking section on pages 20-27. It's short and worth reading, even if you learn only one new thing that you didn't know before.

The Units

All the quilts in this book were made using the simple units shown below. On page 8, you will get a more detailed look at how these units can be combined to create blocks and borders. Directions for piecing the units begin on page 12.

> Scale: Each square equals 1½".
>
> The unit sizes on pages 7 through 14 are finished dimensions.

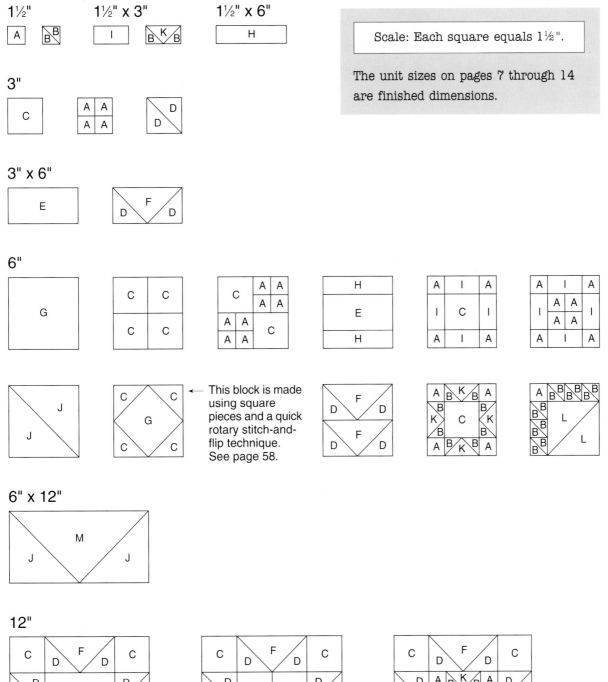

1½" A B/B

1½" x 3" I B K B

1½" x 6" H

3"

3" x 6"

6"

← This block is made using square pieces and a quick rotary stitch-and-flip technique. See page 58.

6" x 12"

12"

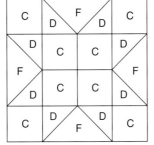

Using the Units

Four 1½" squares can be used to make a 3" unit.

Similarly, you can choose four 3" units
and put them together to make a 6" block.

Any of the 6" units
can be used alone
or as the center of
a 12" star block.

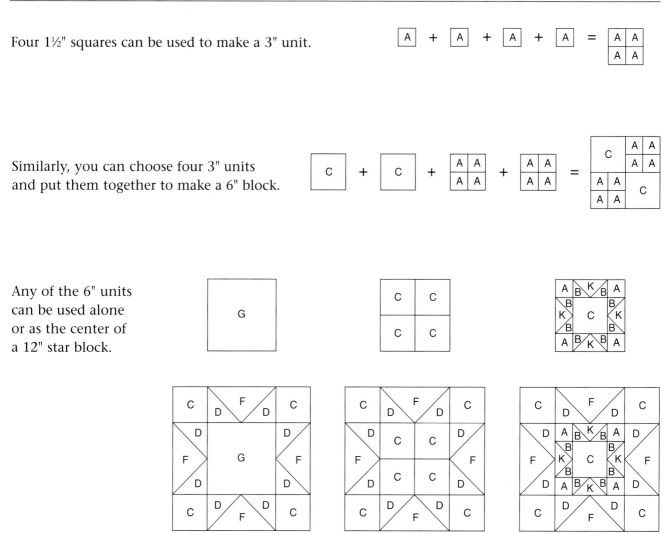

I kept to the same standard measurements when I added borders to my quilts. This makes it easy
to use units and blocks in the borders. Here, 6" star blocks are added to the ends of a 6"-wide border.
(See "Colette" on page 48.)

A random collection of 3" units and 3" x 6" units, combined with 6" star blocks, makes a beautiful
pieced border. (See "Arabella" on page 40.)

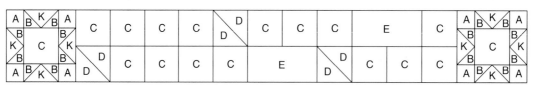

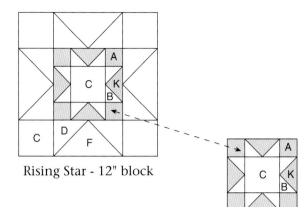

Rising Star - 12" block

Evening Star - 6" block

Additional Blocks

These blocks can be substituted for any 6" block used in the featured quilts.

Birds in the Air

Windmill

Broken Dishes

Square in a Square

King's Crown

Shoofly

Quilter's Surprise

Yankee Puzzle

Broken Sash

Pinwheel

Crosses and Losses

Indian Star

Ribbon Star

The Mayflower

Sharon's 6-Patch

Union Square

Scale: Each square equals 1½".
"On point" diagonal set

Scale: Each square equals 1½".
Straight set

Template Cutting Technique

Press seams in direction of arrows. (Rotary cutting instructions for pieces A-L are on page 18.)

1½" finished units

To make this unit:	Cut:	Assemble:
	1 Template A.	
	2 Template B.	

3" finished units

To make this unit:	Cut:	Assemble:
	1 Template C.	
	4 Template A.	
	2 Template D.	

3" x 6" finished units

To make this unit:	Cut:	Assemble:
	1 Template E.	
	1 Template F and 2 Template D.	

6" finished units

To make this unit:	Cut:	Assemble:
	1 Template G.	
	4 Template C.	
	2 Template C and 8 Template A.	

6" finished units (continued)

To make this unit:	Cut:	Assemble:

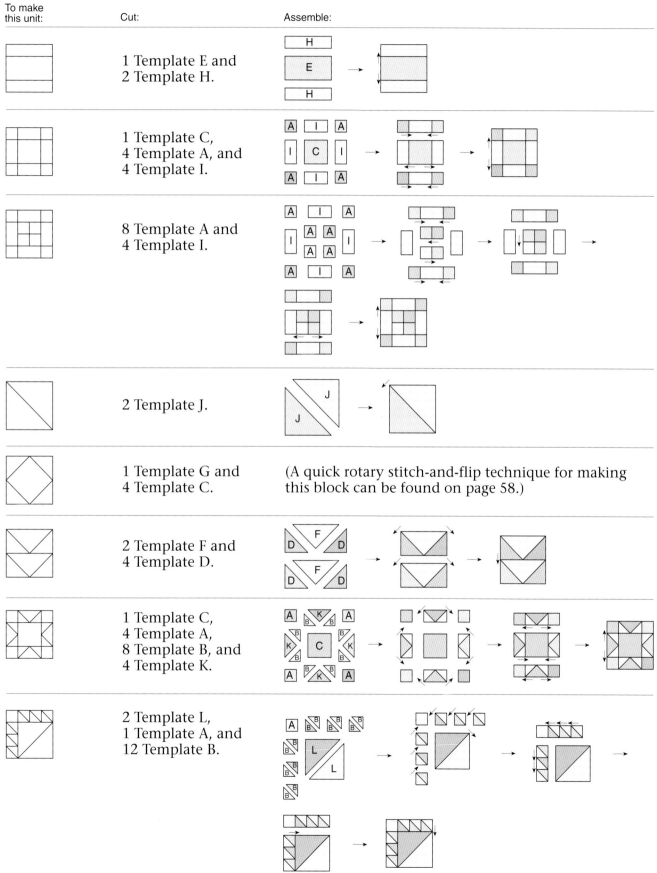

	1 Template E and 2 Template H.	
	1 Template C, 4 Template A, and 4 Template I.	
	8 Template A and 4 Template I.	
	2 Template J.	
	1 Template G and 4 Template C.	(A quick rotary stitch-and-flip technique for making this block can be found on page 58.)
	2 Template F and 4 Template D.	
	1 Template C, 4 Template A, 8 Template B, and 4 Template K.	
	2 Template L, 1 Template A, and 12 Template B.	

6" x 12" finished units

To make this unit:

← Cutting diagram. (Not to scale.)

Cut:

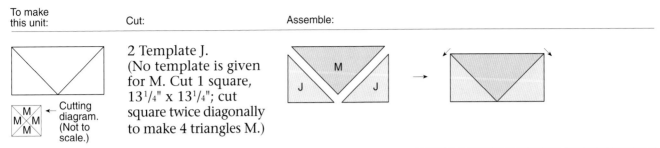

2 Template J.
(No template is given for M. Cut 1 square, 13$^{1}/_{4}$" x 13$^{1}/_{4}$"; cut square twice diagonally to make 4 triangles M.)

Assemble:

12" finished units

To make this unit:

Cut:

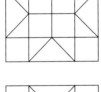

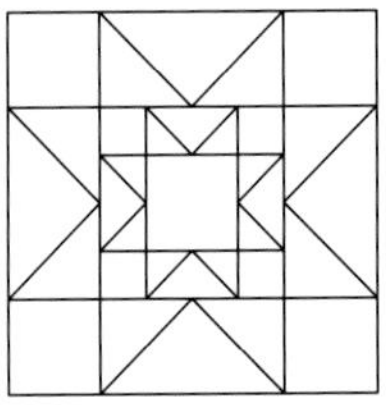

4 template C,
8 template D,
4 template F, and
1 template G.

(Or, instead of template G, use any 6" finished unit for the center of this block.)

Assemble:

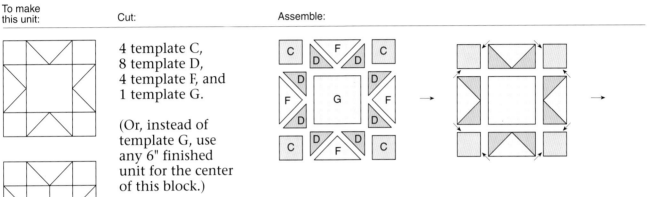

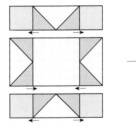

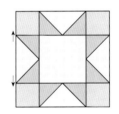

Templates

Template
I
1½" x 3" finished

1/4" seam allowance

straight of grain

1/4" seam allowance

straight of grain

1/4" seam allowance

Template
B

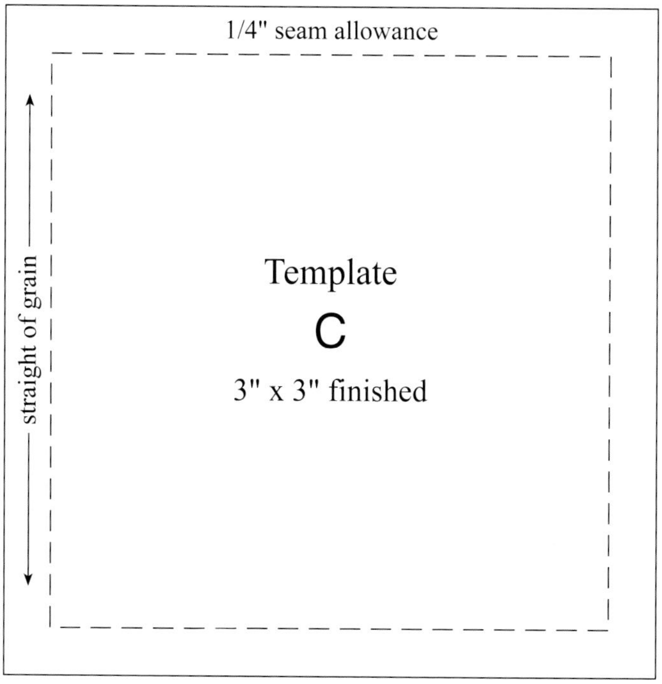

1/4" seam allowance

straight of grain

Template
C
3" x 3" finished

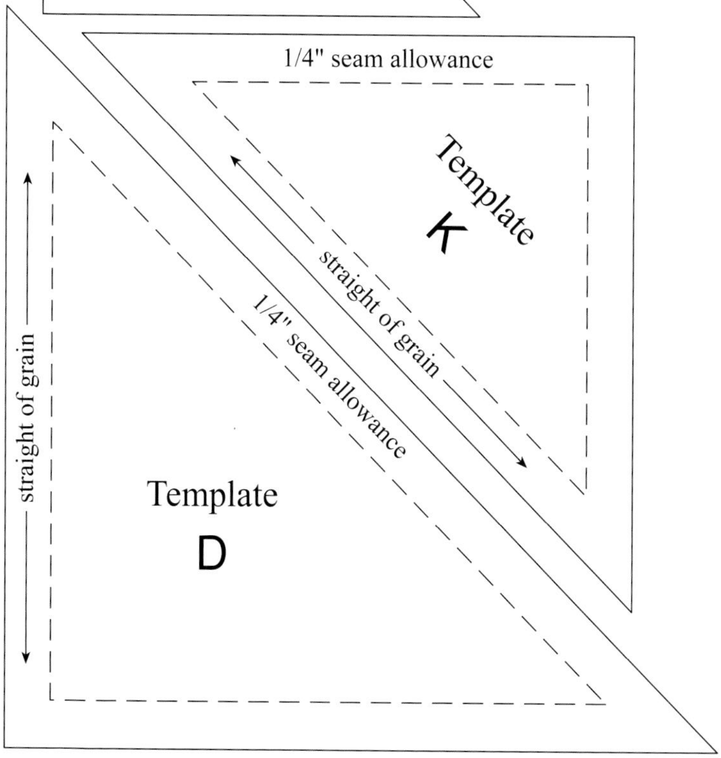

1/4" seam allowance

straight of grain

Template
K

straight of grain

1/4" seam allowance

Template
D

1/4" seam allowance

Template
E
3" x 6" finished

straight of grain

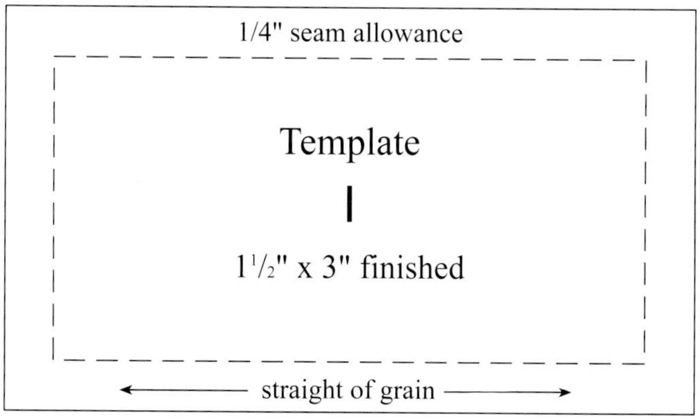

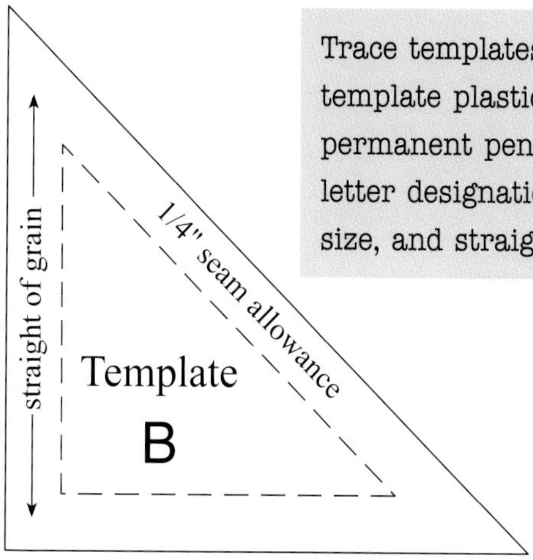

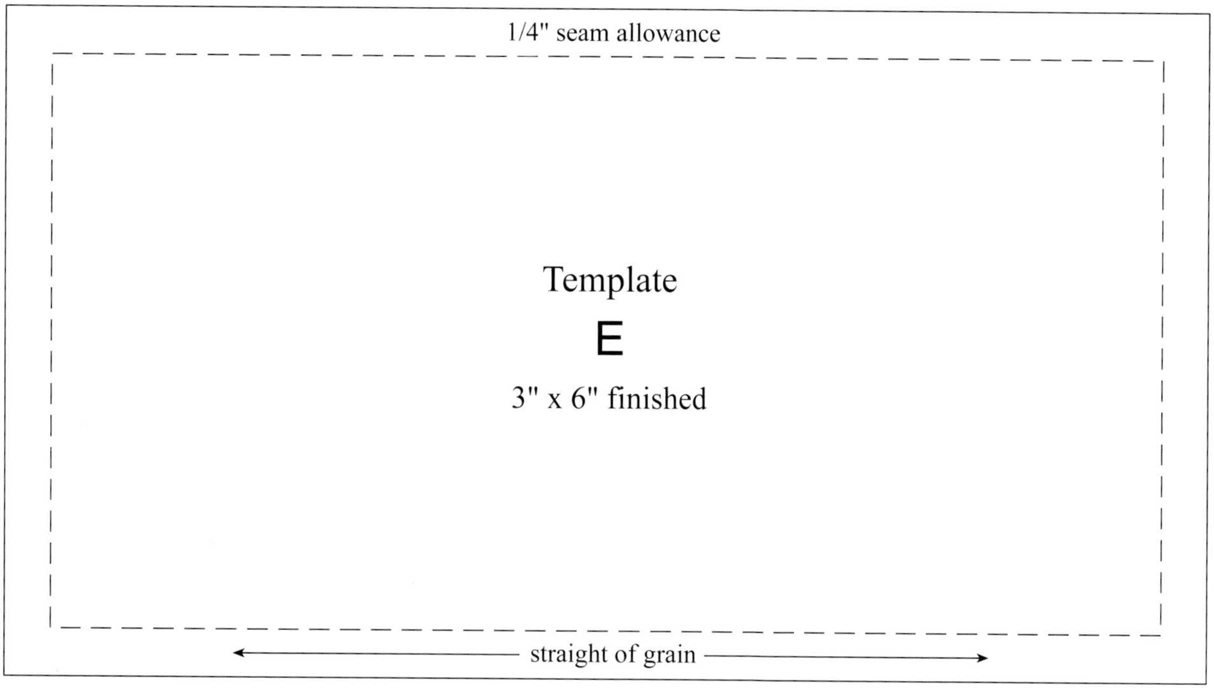

1/4" seam allowance

straight of grain

Template

G

6" x 6" finished

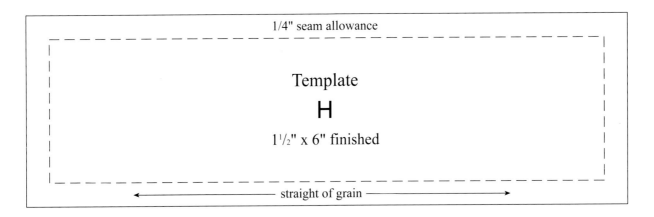

1/4" seam allowance

Template

H

1¹⁄₂" x 6" finished

straight of grain

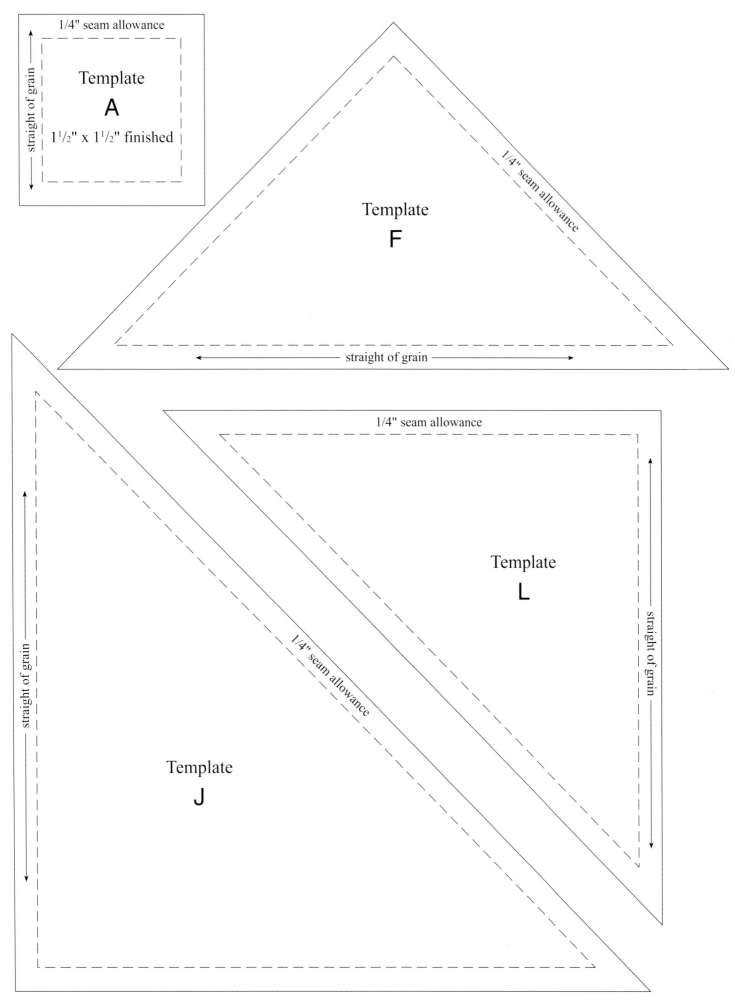

1/4" seam allowance

straight of grain

Template
A

$1^1/_2$" x $1^1/_2$" finished

Template
F

1/4" seam allowance

straight of grain

1/4" seam allowance

Template
L

straight of grain

1/4" seam allowance

straight of grain

Template
J

1/4" seam allowance

Rotary Cutting the Units

Templates are provided, on pages 15-17, for most of the pieces used in the featured quilts. If preferred, you may rotary cut any of the pieces. Below, you will find small diagrams of each template. Next to each diagram are quick rotary cutting instructions for that piece (triangle pieces also show a rotary cutting diagram). (See pages 22-23 for basic rotary cutting instructions.)

Template A

Cut square, 2" x 2".

Template B

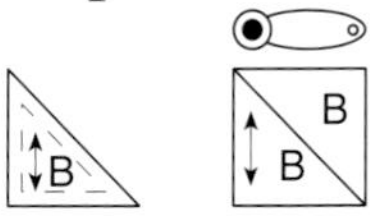

Cut square, 2⅜" x 2⅜"; cut square once diagonally to make 2 of triangle B.

Template C

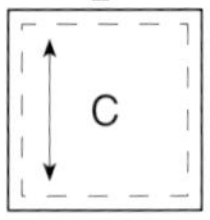

Cut square, 3½" x 3½".

Template D

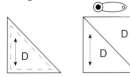

Cut square, 3⅞" x 3⅞"; cut square once diagonally to make 2 of triangle D.

Template K

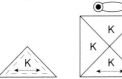

Cut square, 4¼" x 4¼"; cut square twice diagonally to make 4 of triangle K.

Template L

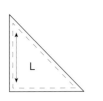

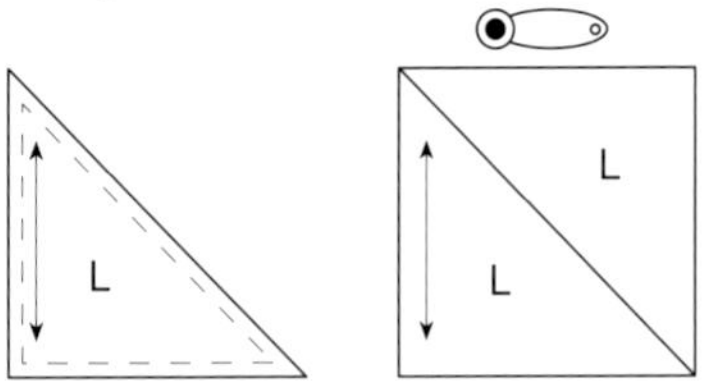

Cut square, 5⅜" x 5⅜"; cut square once diagonally to make 2 of triangle L.

Template G

Cut square, 6½" x 6½".

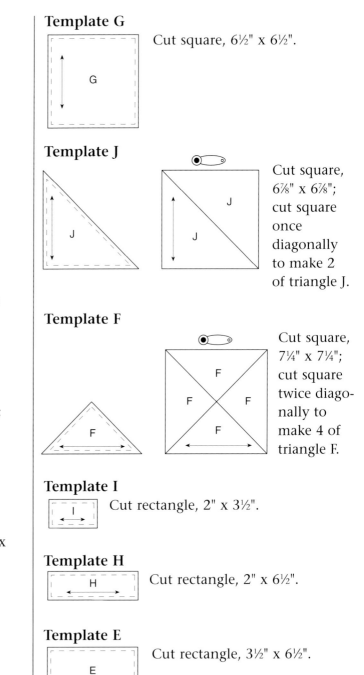

Template J

Cut square, 6⅞" x 6⅞"; cut square once diagonally to make 2 of triangle J.

Template F

Cut square, 7¼" x 7¼"; cut square twice diagonally to make 4 of triangle F.

Template I

Cut rectangle, 2" x 3½".

Template H

Cut rectangle, 2" x 6½".

Template E

Cut rectangle, 3½" x 6½".

Using Triangle Units

I have used 6" and 12" star blocks in many of the quilts in this book. The star block is made up of squares, half-square triangles, and quarter-square triangles.

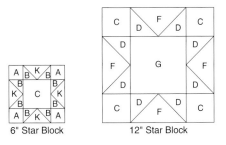

6" Star Block   12" Star Block

Read the discussion of "Fabric Grain" on pages 20-21, to understand why grain direction is important in avoiding stretched edges and distortion in your quilts.

A **half-square triangle** is literally one-half of a square; the square is cut on the straight-of-grain (lengthwise or widthwise grain) of fabric, and then is cut once diagonally, from corner to corner. The resulting two triangles have the straight-of-grain along their short sides. In our star block examples, the star points (pieces B and D) are made of half-square triangles.

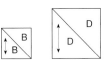

Notice that, when placed in position in the block, the straight grain of the triangles runs vertically and horizontally across the block.

Quilt blocks are most stable, and less prone to stretching out of shape, when the straight-of-grain consistently runs vertically and horizontally across the length and width of the block.

A **quarter-square triangle** is literally one-fourth of a square; the square is cut on the straight-of-grain (lengthwise or widthwise grain) of fabric, and then is cut twice diagonally, from corner to corner. The resulting four triangles have the straight-of-grain along their long side.

The background triangles, (pieces K and F) in our star block examples, are made of quarter-square triangles.

 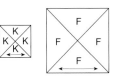

Notice again that, when placed in the block, the straight grain of the background triangles runs vertically and horizontally across the block.

All of the quilt instructions in this book include rotary cutting directions for cutting the half-square triangles and quarter-square triangles needed for making the quilts exactly as they are shown. If, in making one of the quilts, you decide to substitute half-square triangles or quarter-square triangles for a square piece, follow these guidelines:

To make half-square triangles, start with the finished size of the square (in these patterns, the squares are commonly 1½", 3", or 6"). Add ⅞" for seam allowance. Cut out a square, then cut once diagonally, from corner to corner, to make two half-square triangles. See example below.

Half-square triangles

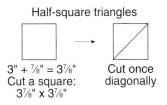

3" + ⅞" = 3⅞"
Cut a square:
3⅞" x 3⅞"

Cut once diagonally

To make quarter-square triangles, start with the finished size of the square (in these patterns, the squares are commonly 1½", 3", or 6"). Add 1¼" for seam allowance. Cut out a square, then cut twice diagonally, from corner to corner, to make four half-square triangles. See example below.

Quarter-square triangles

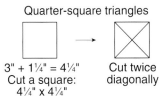

3" + 1¼" = 4¼"
Cut a square:
4¼" x 4¼"

Cut twice diagonally

Basic Quiltmaking

Supplies

- **Sewing machine.** A well-tuned machine with a good straight stitch is all that's needed for piecing your quilt top. If you plan to machine quilt your top, you'll need a walking foot (for straight-line quilting), or a darning foot (for free-motion quilting).
- **Iron and ironing board.** Small tabletop boards are ideal for these small quilts.
- **Rotary cutter.** Pick one that fits your hand comfortably. The 45mm blade is a good size for most quilting applications. I like the small 28mm blade for cutting individual shapes.
- **Rotary mat.** You'll need one that's at least 18" x 24". If you have the space, a 24" x 36" mat is ideal.
- **Acrylic rulers** for rotary cutting. Handy ruler sizes for the quilts in this book are 3" x 18" and 6" x 12" for cutting strips and rectangles; 6½" x 6½" for cutting smaller pieces; and 12½" x 12½" for cutting larger pieces. We recommend the 3½" x 3½" and 6½" x 6½" Precision Trimmer™ rulers by Marsha McCloskey. These work beautifully for trimming your blocks.
- **Fabric grips.** These are small, sandpaper circles that you can stick to your templates or rulers to keep them from slipping while marking or cutting.
- **Template plastic.** Packages of template plastic, usually in 8½" x 11" sheets, are available at quilt shops.
- **Permanent marking pen.** Use for tracing templates and markings onto template plastic.
- **Work wall.** It is important that Blended Quilts are constructed on a vertical surface so you can identify the color movement, value placement, and overall design. I recommend flannel, thin batting, felt, or a product called Quilt Wall® available at many quilt shops. The advantage of Quilt Wall® is the 72" x 72" size and its holding power.
- **Scissors.** Three pairs are optimal: one for cutting fabric, one for cutting template plastic, and a small pair for snipping threads.
- **Pins.** Sharp straight pins are essential for pinning seams. A magnetic pin holder comes in handy here. Have on hand rustproof safety pins if you plan to pin-baste the quilt top, batting, and backing together prior to quilting.
- **Seam ripper.** It's good for ripping seams, and also helpful in steering smaller pieces of fabric through the sewing machine.
- **Tape measure.** You'll need this to measure your quilt top, prior to cutting your quilt borders.
- **Marking tool** (optional) for marking quilting lines.
- **Stencils** (optional) for marking quilting lines.
- **Yardstick** (optional) for marking quilting lines.

Fabric Tips

Prewashing Fabric

There is divided opinion on whether or not it is desirable to prewash your fabric before using it in your quilts. Some quilters prefer to keep the crisp look of their brand new fabric, and opt not to prewash it, particularly if they are making wall quilts which they don't anticipate laundering in the future. If you do plan to wash your completed quilt, it is probably best to prewash all of your fabric prior to sewing. If the fabric is going to shrink, it's best to have it shrink before it's in your quilt! (Washing a quilt that is made of fabric that has not been prewashed, may result in uneven shrinkage.) Wash your new fabric in warm water, with mild detergent (or no detergent, if preferred). Tumble dry on warm cycle. Press gently with a hot iron on steam setting. Take care not to stretch the fabric.

Fabric Grain

A basic knowledge of fabric grain is important to the success of your quilt. If you are unfamiliar with the terms: selvage, lengthwise grain, widthwise grain, straight-of-grain, and bias, read this section!

Study a yard of fabric. You'll see two *selvages*, the densely woven ½" to ¾" sections — sometimes with writing or color bars — which finish the edges of the fabric. Fabric has *lengthwise grain* (threads running the length of the fabric, parallel to the selvage), and *widthwise grain* (threads running the width of the fabric, perpendicular to the selvage). Both lengthwise and widthwise grains are considered *straight-of-grain*. If you tug the fabric along the lengthwise grain, you'll notice that there is very little stretching. The widthwise grain is slightly stretchier. Stretchiest of all is the *bias*, which refers to the diagonal of the fabric (45° from the straight-of-grain).

It is always best to cut quilt pieces on the straight-of-grain. This is easy with squares and rectangles. Half-square triangles are cut with two edges on straight-of-grain, and one edge on bias. Quarter-square triangles are cut with one edge on straight-of-grain, and two edges on bias. Following the rotary instructions for each quilt will ensure that your pieces are on the correct grain. If using templates, be sure to mark the grain-line arrow on your template, then match it to the straight grain of your fabric.

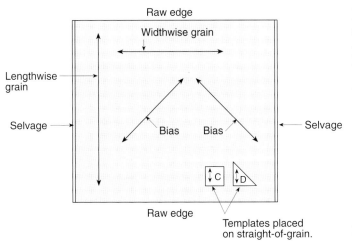

Raw edge
Widthwise grain
Lengthwise grain
Selvage
Bias Bias
Selvage
C D
Raw edge
Templates placed on straight-of-grain.

It is a good idea to remove selvage edges before cutting strips for a project, so that the tough edge, or writing, are not included in your measurement (or your quilt).

Two Cutting Techniques

You can choose between templates or rotary techniques when cutting the pieces for your quilt. An overview of both is given below.

Templates

Templates are given (on pages 15-17) for all of the common pieces used to make the quilts in this book. With a permanent marking pen, carefully trace each template onto template plastic. Also copy each grain-line arrow and letter designation onto the template plastic. Cut out templates with paper-cutting scissors (don't use your best fabric-cutting scissors for this job!) Place templates on right side of fabric, matching arrows to straight grain of fabric. Trace around template with permanent pen; then cut on marked line with fabric scissors, or with rotary cutter and acrylic ruler. *Note:* You will position templates on right side of fabric, so you can view the position of the motifs underneath.

Selective Cutting

For added appeal, you might want to feature a few pictorial prints in the 3" and 6" finished squares (pieces C and G) in your quilt. To selectively cut pictorial prints, first make a see-through cutting template from template plastic. Mark the ¼" seam allowance on your template. Place the template on your fabric and center your chosen motif within the marked seam allowances. Draw around the template with a permanent pen; then cut on the marked line with fabric scissors, or with rotary cutter and acrylic ruler.

If you are making a quilt with blocks set "on point," make sure that you take this into account when selectively cutting squares from a pictorial print. Placing your template "on point" on the print will ensure that the figures will be right-side-up when sewn into your quilt (see "Gloria" on page 64).

Rotary Cutting Basics

If you are new to rotary cutting, practice on scrap fabric first.

Always remember to:

- Keep your fingers and other body parts away from the blade (it's very sharp).
- Close the blade each time you finish cutting. This is a very important habit to get into.
- Keep the cutter out of the reach of children.

Cutting Strips

Fold the fabric selvage to selvage, aligning the widthwise and lengthwise grains as best you can. Place fabric on the rotary cutting mat with the folded edge closest to you. Align a square plastic cutting ruler with the fold of the fabric and place a long cutting ruler to the left.

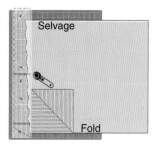

When making all cuts, fabric should be placed to your right. (If you are left handed, reverse the directions.) Remove the square plastic cutting ruler and cut along the right side of the long ruler to trim away the uneven raw edges of fabric. Be sure to hold the long ruler firmly in place, and roll the cutter away from you, cutting through all layers.

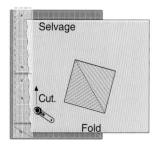

Make successive cuts measuring from the first cut. Refer to the quilt directions for the correct strip width. Position the ruler so that the strip width measurement (2" for example) is aligned with the cut edge of your fabric. Cut strip.

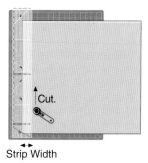

Some of the quilts in this book call for lengthwise border strips. Position the fabric so cuts will be parallel to the selvage. For your first cut, evenly trim away the selvage (approximately ¾"). Refer to quilt directions for correct strip width, then make successive cuts measuring from the first cut.

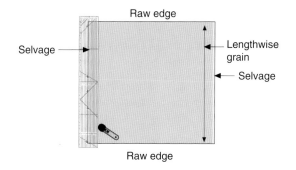

Border Strips

Always cut, or at least plan, your borders first — allowing plenty of length — if you will be using small pieces of the same fabric in the blocks of your quilt. It's so easy to cut into the length of a fabric and then realize your borders are too short!

Don't let this happen to a large exquisite print, or you may have to make other plans for your border.

Squares and Rectangles

Generally, it is easiest to cut a strip first, then to crosscut your squares or rectangles from that strip. Strips are generally cut across the width of fabric. Because the quilts in this book are scrap quilts, you may need only one or two pieces of a fabric. Determine your needs before you cut into the cloth. You may want to cut only individual squares and rectangles.

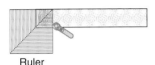
Ruler

See page 18 for instructions on rotary cutting triangles.

Machine Piecing

Use 100% cotton thread or European polyester thread, which is cross-wound on the spool. Most quilters choose one color of thread, and use it to piece the whole quilt regardless of color changes in the fabric. If most of your prints are light to medium in value, an ecru or light gray thread is a good choice. For a predominantly dark quilt, consider dark gray, navy, brown, or black thread.

Sew scant ¼" seams. On some machines the width of the presser foot is ¼" and can be used as guide. If you don't have such a foot, you will need to establish the proper seam allowance on your sewing machine. Place a piece of quarter-inch graph paper under the presser foot and gently lower the needle next to the line that is ¼" from the edge of the paper. Lay a piece of masking tape at the edge of the paper to act as the ¼" guide. Always try to go smaller, rather than larger. If your seams are not exact, narrower is a better choice.

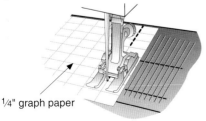
¼" graph paper

For the patterns in this book, sew from cut edge to cut edge. Backtacking is generally unnecessary.

Chain Piecing

Chain piecing is a great time-saver.
1. Sew the first set of pieces together and continue stitching off the edge for a few stitches, creating a "chain" of thread.
2. Without lifting the presser foot, arrange the next set of pieces and feed it under the foot while you sew. Continue in this manner until all of your sets have been stitched.
3. Clip the threads between the stitched units.

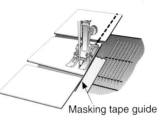
Masking tape guide

Pinning

Pin seams before stitching if matching is involved, or if your seams are longer than 4". Pin points of matching (where seam lines or points meet) first. Once these important points are in place, pin the rest of the seam, easing if necessary (see Easing on page 24).

Pressing

In this book, most seams are pressed to one side, toward the darker fabric whenever possible. Sometimes, for matching purposes, seams are pressed in opposite directions, regardless of which is the darker fabric.

Press with a dry iron that has a shot of steam when needed. Take care not to overpress. Aim for an up-and-down "pressing" motion, rather than a back-and-forth "ironing" motion. Overly vigorous ironing will stretch and distort your piecing. A good pressing technique is first to press the sewn seam flat to "set" it.

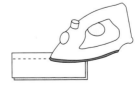

Next, fold the top piece back, covering the seam allowances, and press along the seam line. Gently press and lift your iron without stretching the seam.

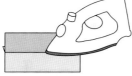

Finally, turn over your piece and press the wrong side of the fabric.

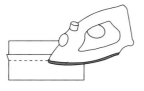

Check Your Work

Piecing a quilt top is always easier if you are accurate and check your work as you go along. Many of our quilts use pieced units (half-square triangle units and fourpatches) that finish at 3" or 6". This means that before these units are sewn to other pieces, they should measure exactly 3½" or 6½" from raw edge to raw edge.

Use Marsha McCloskey's Precision Trimmer 3™ or Precision Trimmer 6™ to check your work. Center the ruler on the pieced units as pictured and trim the edges to make perfect 3½" or 6½" squares.

Matching

1. **Opposing seams.** This is arguably the most important matching technique in quiltmaking! If you use this method, your seams will match when joining units and rows of blocks. When stitching one seamed unit to another, press seam allowances on seams that need to match in opposite directions. The two "opposing" seams will hold each other in place and evenly distribute the bulk.

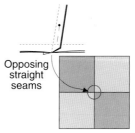

Opposing straight seams

Often, the opposing seams are diagonal seams. Always plan pressing to take advantage of opposing seams.

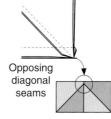

Opposing diagonal seams

2. **Positioning pin.** Carefully push a pin straight through two points that need to match. Pull the pin tight to establish the proper point of matching. Pin the seam normally and remove the positioning pin before stitching.

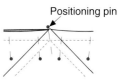

Positioning pin

3. **The X.** When triangles are pieced, stitches will form an X at the next seam line. Stitch through the center of the X to make sure the points on the sewn triangles will not be chopped off.

The X

4. **Easing.** When two pieces to be sewn together are supposed to match but instead are slightly different lengths, pin the points of matching and lightly steam press the seam before stitching. Stitch with the shorter piece on top. The feed dog eases the fullness of the bottom piece.

Easing

Setting the Quilt Blocks Together

Each quilt pattern has a Quilt Assembly Diagram showing how the blocks and setting pieces (large squares, side- and corner-setting triangles, or sashing strips) will be sewn together in rows. When sewing the rows together, press for opposing seams and pin all points of matching.

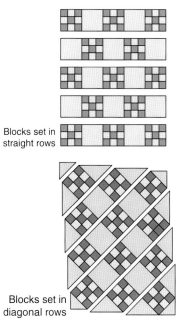

Blocks set in straight rows

Blocks set in diagonal rows

Borders

The borders for all of the quilts in this book were cut and attached to the sides first, then to the top and bottom edges of the quilt top. Applying borders in this order allows you to buy the least amount of fabric.

1. To cut the two side borders to the right length, measure the quilt top length (including seam allowances) through the center. Cut two strips to this measurement. This method of measuring and cutting helps prevent waviness in your border. (If the sides of your quilt top are longer than the center, they will have to be eased into the border. This will prevent rippling in your quilt top.)
2. Mark the center and quarter points on both the quilt top and border strips.
3. Matching ends, centers, and quarter points, pin border strips to the quilt top. Pin generously and press along the matched edges to set the seam before sewing. A shot of steam will help with any easing that might be required.
4. Using a ¼" seam allowance, stitch the border to the quilt top. Press the seam allowance to one side as directed in the quilt instructions.
5. Repeat steps 1-4 to measure the quilt width (including the borders just added), cut, and attach the top and bottom borders.

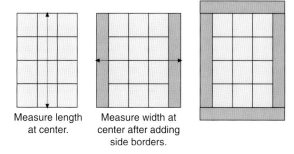

Measure length at center.

Measure width at center after adding side borders.

Finishing Your Quilt

Backing

The rule of thumb for wall quilt backings is that they should measure 4" wider and 4" longer than your quilt top. This gives you an ample working margin while you do your quilting. For quilts that measure more than 36" wide, you'll need to cut your backing fabric into lengths, which should then be sewn together along the long sides. You can sew two lengths together with one center seam, or split the second length and sew the pieces to each side of the first length of fabric. Press seam open.

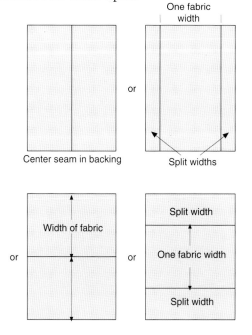

One fabric width

Center seam in backing

Split widths

Width of fabric

Split width

One fabric width

Split width

Batting

Batting dimensions are given in the yardage requirements of each quilt pattern. To achieve the antique look of the quilts shown, choose a low-loft 100% cotton, or 80% cotton/20% polyester, batting. If you prefer 100% polyester batting, be aware that it will give a slightly puffier look to your quilt.

Plan and Mark Quilting Designs

Quilting lines should be evenly distributed over the quilt surface. Directions that come with your batting will tell how close the quilting lines should be to keep the batting from coming apart when the quilt is washed. Avoid tight complicated designs that then require similar quilting over the whole quilt. Likewise avoid leaving large areas unquilted.

You will need a yardstick if you plan to mark long straight quilting lines. For a variety of straight and curved motifs, be sure to check out your local quilt shop's supply of stencils. Your choice of marking tools includes pencils, water-erasable pens, chalk pouncers, and more. No matter what kind of marking tool you choose, light lines will be easier to remove than heavy ones.

Some quilt designs don't require marking. "Stitching in the ditch" is a technique that closely follows seam lines; outline quilting is usually stitched approximately ¼" from seams, allowing you (if machine quilting) to use your machine's foot as a guide.

Layering the Quilt

1. Place the backing, face down, on a large, flat surface and smooth it out so there are no wrinkles. Use masking tape to hold it in place. The backing should be flat and slightly taut, but not stretched off grain.
2. Gently lay the batting on top of the backing, centering and smoothing it as you go.

3. Center the completed quilt top on top of the batting. Starting in the middle, gently smooth out fullness to the sides and corners. Take care not to distort the straight lines of the quilt design and the borders.
4. Use safety pins to hold the layers together, spacing them no more than a hand's width apart, or hand baste through all layers in the pattern shown, using light-colored thread (dark colors may bleed onto your quilt top when you remove them).

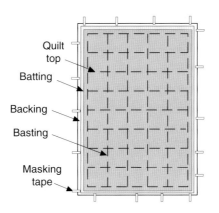

Quilting

All of the quilts in this book were quilted by machine, but they are equally suited to hand quilting. In fact, because of their small size, they would make relaxing and "doable" projects for handwork. Machine quilting and hand quilting are huge subjects. If this is your first quilt, be sure to check your quilt shop or library for some of the excellent books entirely devoted to the topic. Then dive in!

After quilting, machine-baste close to the quilt's edge, through all three layers. Trim excess batting and backing even with the edge of the quilt top. A rotary cutter and long acrylic ruler will ensure accurate straight edges.

Binding

1. Cut binding strips 2½" wide, across the width of fabric (approx. 40" wide). Join the strips together using diagonal seams as shown. Make enough continuous binding to go around the four sides of the quilt plus 6" to 10" for overlap.

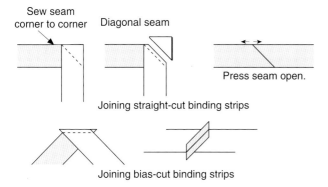

Sew seam corner to corner   Diagonal seam

Press seam open.

Joining straight-cut binding strips

Joining bias-cut binding strips

2. Fold the binding in half lengthwise with wrong sides together and press, taking care not to stretch it. At one end, open out the fold and turn the raw edge in at a 45° angle. Press. Trim, leaving a ¼" seam allowance.

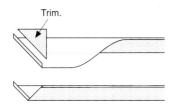

Trim.

3. Beginning on one edge of the quilt a few inches from a corner, pin the binding to the quilt top. Beginning two inches from the folded end of the binding, stitch ⅜" from the raw edges and stop ⅜" from the raw edge at the corner. Backstitch and remove the quilt.

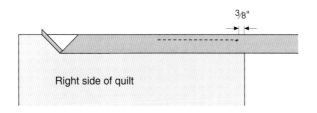

⅜"

Right side of quilt

4. Fold the binding back on itself to create a 45° angle, then turn the binding down to make a fold in the binding that is in line with the upper raw edge of the quilt top. Pin. Stitch the binding to the quilt, ending ⅜" from the next corner. Backstitch and miter the corner as you did the previous one.

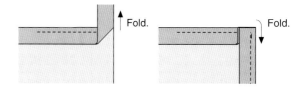

Fold.   Fold.

5. Continue in this manner until the binding has been stitched to all four edges of the quilt top. When you reach the beginning of the binding, trim away excess, leaving 1" to tuck into the folded binding. Complete the stitching.

6. Turn the binding to the back of the quilt and hand sew in place, mitering corners as shown.

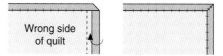

Wrong side of quilt

Color

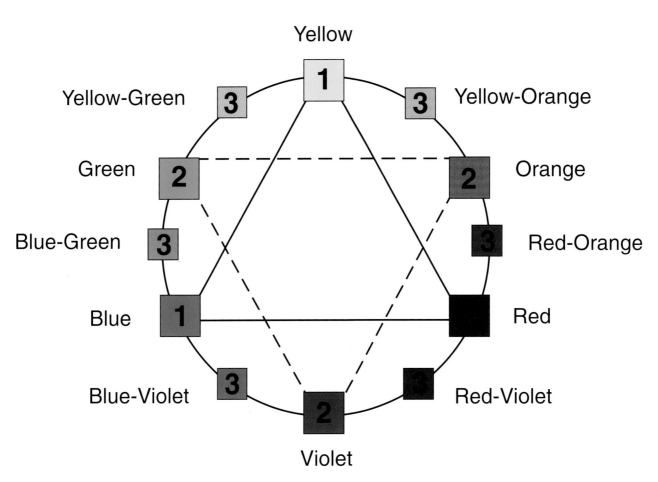

The numbers on the color wheel above correspond to the numbers on the opposite page and the definitions below. This makes it easy for you to identify color groupings for your quilts.

1. Primary colors: yellow, red, blue.

2. Secondary colors: orange, violet (purple), green. These colors are created by mixing parts of two primary colors.

3. Intermediate colors: yellow-orange, red-orange, red-violet, blue-violet, blue-green, yellow-green. These colors are created by mixing equal parts of a primary and its closest secondary color.

The color wheel shows the pure hues of colors. These can be changed by value which is the lightness or darkness of a color. If you add white, gray, or black to a pure hue, you change its value to light (white), medium (gray), or dark (black). For instance, the primary colors—yellow, red, and blue—might look like this.

Study the color chart on the next page and relate the values to their place on the color wheel.

Color Chart

Cool Colors

SHADE	TONE	TINT	HUE

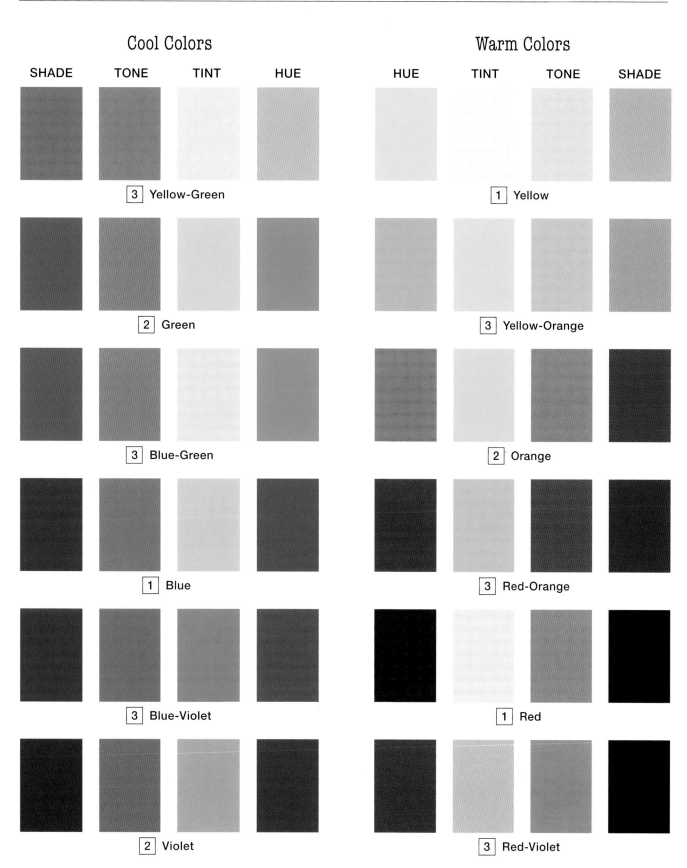

3 Yellow-Green

2 Green

3 Blue-Green

1 Blue

3 Blue-Violet

2 Violet

Warm Colors

HUE	TINT	TONE	SHADE

1 Yellow

3 Yellow-Orange

2 Orange

3 Red-Orange

1 Red

3 Red-Violet

Color Recipes

Try a color recipe from one of these pages as a start for a wall quilt. Refer to the Color Wheel and Color Chart as you are doing this. You do not have to use the colors shown here.

Read the definitions of different combinations, such as Analogous, Complementary, etc, and pick your own color groupings using the boxed numbers as a reference. Remember, you may use any shade, tone, tint, or hue of a color to create this mixture.

Because Blended Quilts are scrappy, you will be choosing multi-hued prints and will have more colors than those in your color recipe selection. Try to emphasize your chosen colors by adding tonal prints that read like solids. For instance, in #4 Split Complementary, search for fabrics that emphasize blue-green, brown, and red in any intensity. They may be tonals, toiles, florals, plaids or ? Space them throughout your quilt so your color recipe is evident and recognizable.

1. Complementary – Any two colors opposite each other on the color wheel.

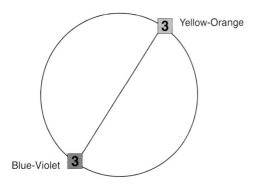

2. Triadic – Any three colors equidistant from each other on the color wheel. (Notice that brown is the darkest shade of orange.)

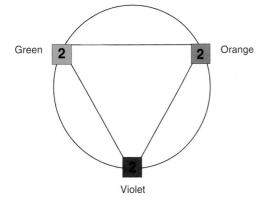

3. Analogous – Any two or three adjoining colors on the color wheel.

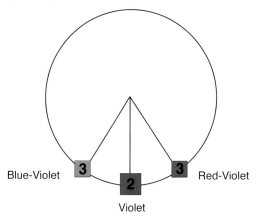

Blue-Violet **3**   **2**   **3** Red-Violet

Violet

4. Split Complementary – The two colors on each side of a color's complement.

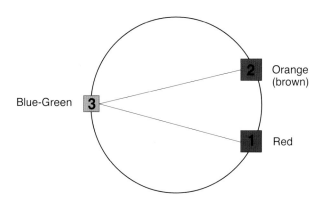

2 Orange (brown)

Blue-Green **3**

1 Red

5. Double Complementary – Any two adjoining colors plus their complements.

Yellow

Yellow-Green **3**   **1**

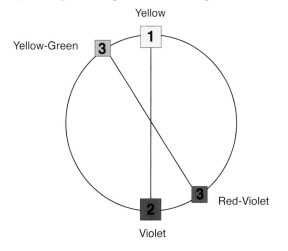

3 Red-Violet

2

Violet

Value and Contrast

Value creates contrast. Value can be light, medium, or dark. This determination depends on adjacent fabrics and their lightness or darkness.

Block #1 - If you put similar values together (in this case, three medium-value fabrics) you will have very low contrast. None of the star points will stand out and the design will be lost as the stars almost disappear. This technique would not be used in traditional quiltmaking, as you would generally use high contrast to make the stars appear, but is an important component of Blended Quilts. The seams between the individual pieces blend into a pattern of florals and vines, and a new textile design seems to appear. This is the type of block that invites people to study a quilt and try to identify its construction secrets.

You won't need every block to be this mysterious, however, as it is important to mix very blended, low-contrast blocks with other value blocks such as the medium-contrast and high-contrast examples pictured next.

Block #2 - In this block, light- and medium-value fabrics are pieced together to create a soft, gentle blending where the star points are easily visible. Medium-contrast blocks are easily understood by the viewer, so it is up to you to make intriguing color and fabric choices to hold his or her interest. In this example, the star points are composed of fabrics with a shade of difference, and the center large-floral vine flows into the adjoining pieces.

Block #3 - The high-contrast example is the most traditional block of the group. The star points are a very dark value, causing them to stand out and contrast with the light fabrics that surround them. If you create a quilt with all high-contrast star blocks you would have to work very hard at selecting your surrounding pieces to achieve an overall blended look. Generally, high-contrast blocks are used as accents throughout a Blended Quilt.

Block #3

After you consider lightness and darkness and how value determines the look of your quilt, let's continue on to the category of warm and cool colors. Look at the color chart on page 29 to identify the choices below. Study the colors and play with some fabrics to see how colors react to each other to advance and recede. Advancing colors will be accents in your quilt and should be distributed across your top for greatest design impact. Use these colors to emphasize an area or element.

Study the effect you can obtain by placing a cool color next to a warm color. This is a color contrast you need in order to add sparkle to your quilt.

These Colors Advance

Hue or pure colors

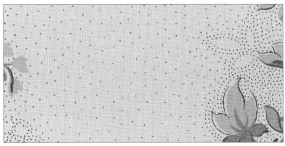

Warm colors - red, yellow, orange

Dark colors

These Colors Recede

Grayed colors

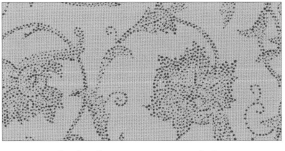

Cool colors - green, gray, beige

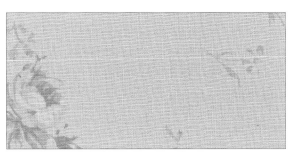

Light colors

Fabric Choice

The secret to creating the pretty, luxurious look of early English, French, Dutch, and American quilts is in your fabric and color choices. There are some very specific fabrics that make these quilts unique, including:

- Large, spaced florals or floral bouquet prints.
- Toile designs.
- Medium floral prints with an antique "French" look, many containing designs of curved vines, ribbons, and birds. The motifs should be spaced, with a large amount of background showing.

Texture is a very important element that helps to give a quilt depth and body. Search for interesting reproduction fabrics. Many have background details such as picotage, shading, multiple patterns, and sponge effects. Watch for mellow fabrics with tone-on-tone motifs for your quiet spaces. Curved designs are important as they add "flow" to your quilt. Remember, everything can't be excitement. You need many shades and tones of neutrals in supporting roles, allowing the really colorful patterns to sparkle!

In this section, we will examine the fabrics necessary for a spectacular Blended Quilt.

Fabric Types

Medium Prints

Medium Prints. Three- or four-color prints of a medium size are needed for Blended Quilts. Find spaced floral patterns with a large amount of background color showing. Flowing designs with curving flowers and vines are what you need.

Small Prints

Small Prints. One- or two-color small floral prints work well. Stay away from very small multicolor designs. They generally read as busy specks and detract from your composition.

Large Prints

Large Prints. The original chintz floral prints were a polished cotton generally referred to as "furnishing weight" cloth. Many wealthy quiltmakers in the eastern and southern areas of the United States could afford to purchase this fabric for quiltmaking. Less affluent quilters would make do with small amounts of chintz. Chintz or "chintz like" fabrics can be exhilarating when used as wide borders. Many times chintz was purchased for this purpose. Blended Quilts look elegant with a large, light floral chintz used inside the quilt and a different dark floral used as the border.

Picotage Floral

Picotage Floral. The picotage effect was created by using metal pins to make small dots on the fabric surface. This added an element of dimension and shading to the cloth. Look for medium florals with picotage in reproduction fabrics currently on the market.

Spaced Floral

Spaced Floral. These multicolored fabrics are useful for creating a bridge across seam lines. This allows diverse roses and other florals to blend together and create a flowing pattern from block to block.

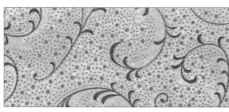

Paisley

Paisley. The curvy, intricate scrollwork designs that we have come to know as paisley originated in India during the 1600s. They are usually multicolored, and their soft curves easily transition into other prints.

Curvilinear Motifs

Curvilinear Motifs. Curved designs can be small to medium with colors that pick up those in multicolored florals. They transition a busy print into a more quiet place. These curved designs are usually tonal and neutral.

Tone-on-Tone

Tone-on-Tone. These prints are usually tints, tones, or shades of a color. They mostly read as a solid or a texture from the distance of a few feet. Use these as light or dark accents, or choose a medium value to blend.

Plaid

Plaid. Choose either large or small patterns, preferably containing several colors that blend with other pieces in your quilt. Their straight lines add texture and introduce a rest from all the curves.

Toile de Jouy

Toile de Jouy. This style of copperplate printing reached its glory when the technique was refined about 1770 by Christophe-Phillipe Oberkampf. Pronounced "twahl du zhwee," meaning "fabric of Jouy," these designs are perfect for quilt backgrounds, sashing, or small pieces that need to read as quiet areas.

Stripes (Ombré)

Stripes (Ombré). Many of the stripes in the early 1800s were novelty patterns. Some contained ribbons and flowers while others featured ombré stripes with vines meandering through. An ombré stripe shades from dark to light, which allows the design to blend with adjoining pieces.

Serpentine with Stripes

Serpentine with Stripes. The serpentine pattern was another popular design for quilts and clothing in the 19th century. An ombré design of light and dark adds depth, while the serpentine pattern curves across the surface of the swatch. This type of design, used in small amounts, will add surprise and texture to your composition.

Scenics

Scenics. Large, multicolor scenic designs add a curious and delightful accent when combined with florals and toiles. They are effective when cut in either large or small pieces. Maybe you want a whole scene in a center medallion block, or just a tiny face in a fourpatch block. Either one works, and people love finding little unexpected treasures in a quilt.

Selecting Fabric for Your Blended Quilt

Fabric is the most important element in capturing the essence of the early quilts. It is easiest to first choose one or two multicolored large floral or scenic prints that will work in your quilt and in the borders. This will be your "focus" fabric. Go through your fabric stash and pull out any fabrics you think might blend with the colors in the large prints.

Sort by color and fabric type, i.e., toiles, medium florals, plaids, tonals. You will probably want pieces with different values, and warm and cool colors, distributed throughout your quilt.

Choose fabrics that contain a tint, tone, or shade of color from the focus fabric. Review the fabric types on pages 34-36 and see what's missing from your collection. If you are missing toiles, large florals, small-to-medium spaced florals, and viney designs, a trip to your local quilt and fabric shop might be in order.

Before you leave home, try this:
1. Get a file folder (legal or letter size).
2. Draw 3" and 6" squares onto the folder using templates from the book, or a ruler. Copy other templates you might use onto paper. (Be sure to copy the stitching line of the template, rather than the cutting line.) Cut around shapes you want and trace onto the folder. Cut out the shapes you have drawn on the folder.
3. These shapes will be used as "viewing templates" at the store. Write size and letter designation of each template on the folder under the cutouts.
4. Staple any color choices and fabric swatches from home inside of the folder.
5. At the store, choose suitable bolts of fabric and lay the viewing templates over the bolt. Look for vine designs, florals, interesting textures, and toiles that will blend with each other or complement the large florals.

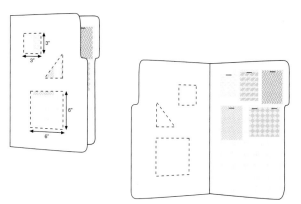

Now that your fabric collection is complete, it is time to play with your choices. Working on a design wall allows you to test color placement and practice with different forms of contrast. It is always a good idea to cut out extra pieces of fabric to audition on the wall. Many times you have to stand back four to six feet to get an accurate read on the design combination. A piece that looks one way one minute may look totally different when other fabrics are placed nearby. Colors in a multicolored fabric may mix to the eye and read differently than they do when alone. Light, medium, and dark values may wash together so no one print is distinct.

In the late 1800s, Impressionist painters such as Claude Monet, Pierre-Auguste Renoir, and Mary Cassatt developed a new style of painting, exploring color and light in ways that captured their feelings about nature and life. They were colorists and one of their most important discoveries was the "broken color technique." When different colors are blended very close to each other, the viewer's eye mixes them and reads them as a color totally different from its components. This makes it difficult to determine how the colors will read.

A design wall gives you the opportunity to place fabrics together until you get the right mix. It also allows you to turn your shapes to see if the pattern flowing in another direction might work better for your design. Study the examples and notice the transitions by size, color, and pattern.

Example 1 - See how the backgrounds and roses in this example blend to create a color wash. Does the pink background warm the blue and make it necessary to use a warmer blue in adjacent fabrics? The green leaves are all different tints, tones, and shades. Is it necessary to find a green that doesn't match any of them to pull the group together? These are choices that can be decided on a design wall and are color exercises that will be helpful to you in all your quiltmaking projects. You may have experienced the "broken color technique" in home decorating projects. You picked a color from a multicolored tweed carpet to use for fabric in your draperies and now they look like they don't match. Although you know they are the same color, the blending of many colors in the carpet has created another tone and has probably made the original color appear warmer or cooler. This is why it's important to "read" the whole pattern repeat, rather than just a small section of color, in a multicolored fabric.

Example 2 - Watch the large multicolored print flowing into a medium print and subtly changing background color and size. The flow continues to another background and size change, and finishes with a two-color design. This flow works because the designs are similar values and contain common colors.

Example 3 - Notice the high contrast and very dissimilar background colors. The floral motifs are similar colors and size so the flow continues in a blended pattern. Your eye reads the design and color and makes an easy transition.

Example 4 - A transition from paisley to a medium floral is accomplished with the use of viney patterns. Notice that the red and brown are very different colors but similar value. The brighter paisley design makes the paisley fabric appear lighter so it transitions to a deeper red before it meets the brown of equal value.

Example 5 - A transition from a light background to a medium background is attained by the use of a floral flow. Because the flowers are warm colors on cool backgrounds they advance and draw your attention away from the backgrounds. Notice, also, how the flowers change from large to small in the flow.

Example 6 - This is a monochromatic color scheme where a gold tonal vine flows into a gold toile design, which then flows into a gold background design, which introduces a red floral that seems to advance because of its brightness.

Now is the time to put what you have learned into practice.
The quilts on the following pages use techniques which have been discussed
in the opening section. Jump in and discover your artistic skills!

Arabella

Materials

Fabric requirements are based on 40" fabric width.

- ¼ yd. *each* of 14 or more assorted prints for blocks and pieced border
- ⅓ yd. coordinating print for inner border
- ½ yd. for binding
- 3¼ yds. for backing
- 50" x 50" batting

Directions

See *Basic Quiltmaking*, beginning on page 20, for general quiltmaking directions. The instructions here are for making "Arabella" exactly as shown. Remember that you can substitute any 6" (finished size) block in place of the star blocks, and any 3" (finished size) unit will work in the pieced border. Choose between two cutting techniques: numbers for both rotary and template cutting are given on the chart below. Templates are on pages 15-17.

A combination of reds, golds, and browns gives this piece a delightful warmth and richness. Lighter blocks are placed near the center to create an inner glow.

Designed by:
Melissa McCulloch

Quilted by:
Margy Duncan

Finished quilt size:
45½" x 45½"

Finished block size:
6" x 6"

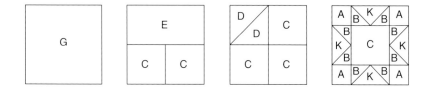

Cutting

Fabric	Piece/Template	Total Needed	Rotary Cutting Technique				
			# to Cut	Shape	1st Cut	2nd Cut	
Assorted prints	G	10	10	☐	6½" x 6½"		
	C	83	83	☐	3½" x 3½"		
	E	8	8	▭	3½" x 6½"		
	D	28	14	☐	3⅞" x 3⅞"	◺	
	A	68	68	☐	2" x 2"		
	K	68	17	☐	4¼" x 4¼"	◻	
	B	136	68	☐	2⅜" x 2⅜"	◺	
Coordinating print	Inner border	2	strips	▭	2" x 30½"		
		2	strips	▭	2" x 33½"		
Binding fabric		5	strips	▭	2½" x 40"		

Block Assembly

All seams ¼". Press seams in direction of arrows unless otherwise instructed.

1. Using 17 of C, and all of A, K, and B pieces, assemble 17 star blocks as shown.

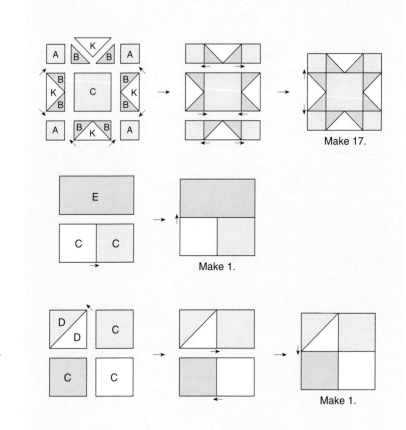

Make 17.

2. Using 5 of C, 1 of E, and 2 of D, make 1 each of 2 alternate blocks.

Make 1.

3. Sew 13 star blocks (remaining 4 will be used in pieced border), 2 alternate blocks, and 10 of G together in horizontal rows as shown in the Quilt Assembly Diagram on page 43. Press away from star blocks. Join rows together. Press seams in one direction.

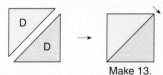

Make 1.

Inner Border

1. Sew the 2" x 30½" strips to sides of quilt top. Press seams toward border.
2. Sew the 2" x 33½" strips to top and bottom of quilt. Press seams toward border.

Make 13.

Pieced Border

1. Sew 26 of D together in pairs.
2. Using D units from Step 1, 61 of C, and 7 of E, make 4 pieced border strips.
3. Sew star blocks to opposite ends of 2 pieced border strips as shown in the Quilt Assembly Diagram on page 43. Press seams toward star blocks.
4. Sew 2 pieced border strips (without star blocks) to sides of quilt top. Press seams toward inner border.
5. Sew 2 pieced border strips (with star blocks) to top and bottom of quilt. Press seams toward inner border.

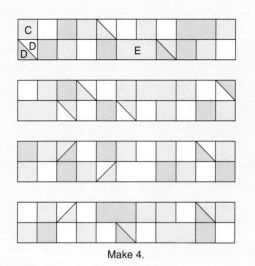

Make 4.

Finishing

1. Cut the backing fabric into two equal lengths and sew long edges together. Press seam open. Trim backing to 50" x 50".
2. Layer quilt top, batting, and backing. Baste layers together.
3. Plan and mark quilting design as desired.
4. Quilt by hand or machine.
5. Trim the batting and backing even with the quilt top edges.
6. Sew the binding strips together to create one long strip. Bind the quilt edges.

Decorating Tip

Use garage sale or inexpensive antique shop finds to add drama or comfort to your wall quilt setting. Notice the tassel used to "dress-up" the yard-sale lamp.

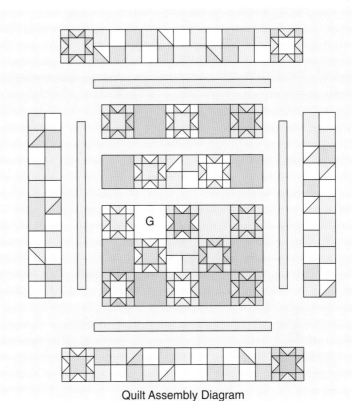

Quilt Assembly Diagram

Each small 6" star is unique. Some stars blend, others contrast, and many of them feature large floral and scenic prints. The red inner border divides the quilt and creates a "stopping" place for the eyes.

Betsy

Materials

Fabric requirements are based on 40" fabric width.

- ¼ yd. *each* of 3 or more assorted blue prints for large star points
- ¼ yd. *each* of 3 or more assorted pink prints for small star points
- ⅓ yd. *each* of 9 or more assorted prints (including large florals) for blocks
- ¼ yd. dark pink print for inner border
- 1¼ yds. floral-swag print for outer border
- ⅝ yd. for binding
- 3⅓ yds. for backing
- 54" x 54" batting

Betsy is so lovely and showcases subtle blending with light floral prints. Blended quilts do not have to be dark and dramatic.

Designed by:
Melissa McCulloch

Quilted by:
Paula Prominski

Finished quilt size:
50" x 50"

Finished block size:
12" x 12"

Directions

See *Basic Quiltmaking*, beginning on page 20, for general quiltmaking directions. Choose between two cutting techniques: numbers for both rotary and template cutting are given on the chart below. Templates are on pages 15-17.

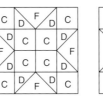

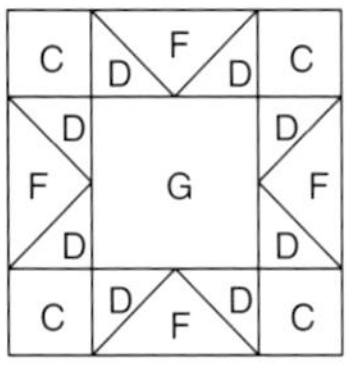

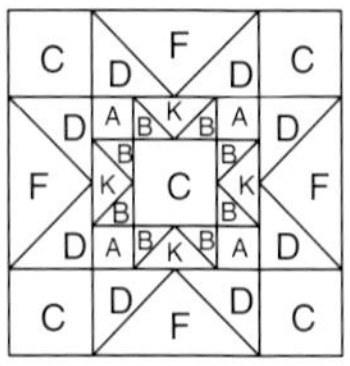

Cutting

Fabric	Piece/Template	Total Needed	Rotary Cutting Technique			
			# to Cut	Shape	1st Cut	2nd Cut
Assorted blue prints	D	72	36	☐	3⅞" x 3⅞"	◺
Assorted pink prints	B	24	12	☐	2⅜" x 2⅜"	◺
Assorted prints (incl. large florals)	F	36	9	☐	7¼" x 7¼"	⊠
	G	3	3	☐	6½" x 6½"	
	C	51	51	☐	3½" x 3½"	
	A	12	12	☐	2" x 2"	
	K	12	3	☐	4¼" x 4¼"	⊠
Dark pink print	Inner border	4	strips	▭	1¼" x 40"*	
Floral-swag print	Outer border	4 length-wise	strips	▭	6½" x 60"**	
Binding fabric		6	strips	▭	2½" x 40"	

*Strips are cut longer than necessary, and will be trimmed to size later.
**Strips are cut long to allow for selective placement of motifs when mitering borders.

Block Assembly

All seams ¼". Press seams in direction of arrows unless otherwise instructed.

1. Using 3 of C, and all of A, K, and B pieces, assemble three 6" star blocks as shown.

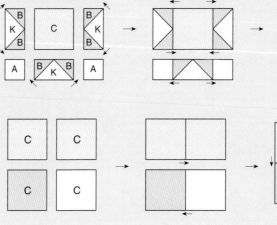

2. Using 12 of C, make 3 fourpatch blocks.

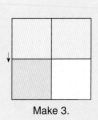

3. Using 36 of C, and all of D, F, and G pieces, and the blocks made in Steps 1 and 2, assemble nine 12" star blocks.

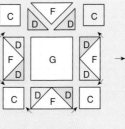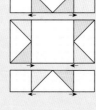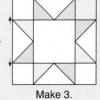

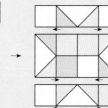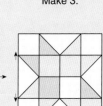

4. Sew 12" star blocks together in horizontal rows as shown in the Quilt Assembly Diagram on page 47. Press for opposing seams. Join rows together. Press seams in one direction.

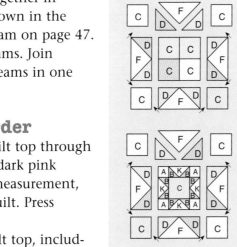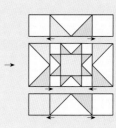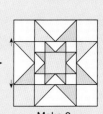

Inner Border

1. Measure length of quilt top through center. Trim 2 of the dark pink border strips to this measurement, and sew to sides of quilt. Press seams toward border.

2. Measure width of quilt top, including borders just added, through center. Trim the remaining 2 dark pink border strips to this measurement, and sew to top and bottom of quilt. Press seams toward border.

Outer Border

1. With right sides together, fold 60"-long floral-swag border strip in half, matching short ends, and lightly crease the center fold. Open

out strip, and find the swag nearest your crease. Find the center of the swag, and mark with a pin. Treat this as the center of your border strip. Repeat with remaining 3 floral-swag border strips.

2. With right sides together, center and sew 2 of the floral-swag border strips to sides of quilt top. Press seams toward borders. The borders will extend beyond the top and bottom of your quilt. Now center and sew remaining 2 floral-swag border strips to top and bottom of quilt; start and stop your seams at the point where the side borders join the quilt top. Miter corner by folding top border under at 45° angle as shown. Hand sew with an invisible stitch, then trim away excess, leaving a ¼" seam allowance. Repeat for each corner.

Please note: *If your swag design is larger or smaller than the one used in our quilt, and you are unhappy with how your corners meet, consider one of these solutions:*

• Appliqué a floral bouquet at each corner.
• Insert a 6" finished square (Template G) at each corner.
• Insert a 6" finished star (see *Arabella,* page 40) at each corner.

Finishing

1. Cut the backing fabric into two equal lengths and sew long edges together. Press seam open. Trim backing to 54" x 54".
2. Layer quilt top, batting, and backing. Baste layers together.
3. Plan and mark quilting design.
4. Quilt by hand or machine.
5. Trim the batting and backing even with the quilt top edges.
6. Sew the binding strips together to create one long strip. Bind the quilt edges.

Wrong side of fabric.
(top border)

Quilt Assembly Diagram

Notice the pretty blending as the flowers cascade diagonally across the star. The flowers are similar colors but the backgrounds change.

Colette

Materials

Fabric requirements are based on 40" fabric width.

- ¼ yd. *each* of 12 or more assorted prints for blocks
- 1 yd. floral print for border
- ½ yd. for binding
- 3 yds. for backing
- 47" x 47" batting

Directions

See *Basic Quiltmaking*, beginning on page 20, for general quiltmaking directions. The instructions here are for making "Colette" exactly as shown. Remember that you can substitute any 6" (finished size) block in place of the center square, and any 3" (finished size) unit will work in the center of the 6" star blocks. Choose between two cutting techniques: numbers for both rotary and template cutting are given on the chart below. Templates are on pages 15-17.

  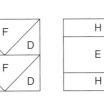

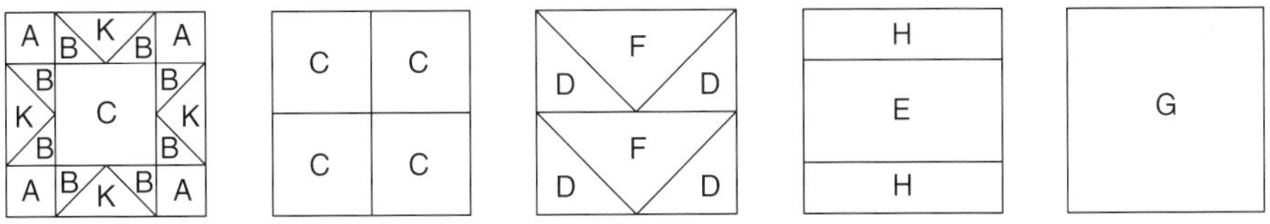

A wonderful collection of large floral and scenic fabrics makes each blended star unique in this elegant quilt. The spare use of red and orange prints gives a welcome touch of sparkle.

Designed by:
Sharon Evans Yenter

Quilted by:
Sherry D. Rogers

Finished quilt size:
42½" x 42½"

Finished block size:
6" x 6"

Cutting

Fabric	Piece/ Template	Total Needed	Rotary Cutting Technique			
			# to Cut	Shape	1st Cut	2nd Cut
Assorted prints	C	28	28	☐	3½" x 3½"	
	A	48	48	☐	2" x 2"	
	K	48	12	☐	4¼" x 4¼"	⊠
	B	96	48	☐	2⅜" x 2⅜"	◹
	D	16	8	☐	3⅞" x 3⅞"	◹
	F	8	2	☐	7¼" x 7¼"	⊠
	E	8	8	▭	3½" x 6½"	
	H	16	16	▭	2" x 6½"	
	G	1	1	☐	6½" x 6½"	
Floral print	Border	4 length-wise	strips	▭	6½" x 30½"	
Binding fabric		5	strips	▭	2½" x 40"	

Block Assembly

All seams ¼". Press seams in direction of arrows unless otherwise instructed.

1. Using 12 of C, and all of A, K, and B pieces, assemble 12 star blocks as shown.

2. Using 16 of C, make 4 fourpatch blocks.

3. Using all of D and F pieces, make 4 flying geese blocks.

4. Using all of E and H pieces, make 8 rail blocks.

5. Sew G piece, 8 star blocks (remaining 4 will be used in border), and all blocks made in Steps 2-4 together in horizontal rows as shown in the Quilt Assembly Diagram on page 51. Press for opposing seams. Join rows together. Press seams in one direction.

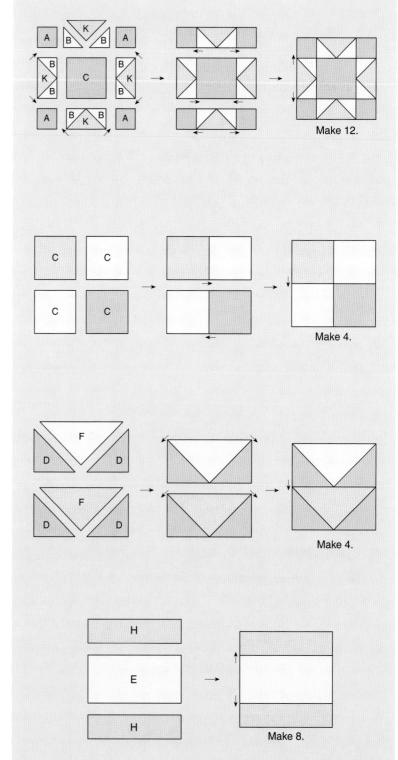

Make 12.

Make 4.

Make 4.

Make 8.

Border

1. Sew star blocks to opposite ends of 2 floral border strips as shown in the Quilt Assembly Diagram. Press seams toward borders.
2. Sew remaining 2 floral border strips to sides of quilt top. Press seams toward borders.
3. Sew 2 floral border strips (with star blocks) to top and bottom of quilt. Press seams toward borders.

Finishing

1. Cut the backing fabric into two equal lengths and sew long edges together. Press seam open. Trim backing to 47" x 47".
2. Layer quilt top, batting, and backing. Baste layers together.
3. Plan and mark quilting design as desired.
4. Quilt by hand or machine.
5. Trim the batting and backing even with the quilt top edges.
6. Sew the binding strips together to create one long strip. Bind the quilt edges.

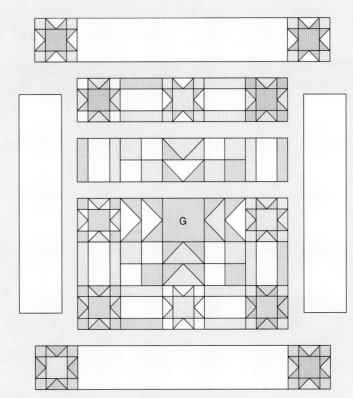

Quilt Assembly Diagram

Decorating Tip

Display your wall quilt on a decorative rod with finials, then accent with a tasseled cord.

Toile fabrics are cut with no consideration to pattern in this quilt. This is reminiscent of the early 1800s, when every piece of toile was a treasure.

Diana

Materials

Fabric requirements are based on 40" fabric width.

- ¼ yd. *each* of 4 or more assorted red prints for blocks
- ¼ yd. *each* of 11 or more assorted beige, tan, and brown prints for blocks
- ½ yd. red floral print for large triangles
- ⅓ yd. light print for inner border
- 1⅔ yds. brown floral print for outer border
- ⅝ yd. for binding
- 3½ yds. for backing
- 56" x 56" batting

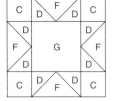

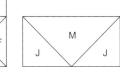

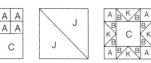

Cutting

Choose between two cutting techniques: numbers for both rotary and template cutting are given on the chart below.

Fabric	Piece/ Template	Total Needed	Rotary Cutting Technique			
			# to Cut	Shape	1st Cut	2nd Cut
Assorted red prints	A	48	48	□	2" x 2"	
	C	4	4	□	3½" x 3½"	
Assorted beige, tan, and brown prints	A	48	48	□	2" x 2"	
	C	28	28	□	3½" x 3½"	
	J	24	12	□	6⅞" x 6⅞"	⧄
	G	1	1	□	6½" x 6½"	
	F	4	1	□	7¼" x 7¼"	⊠
All assorted prints (red, beige, tan, and brown)	D	8	4	□	3⅞" x 3⅞"	⧄
	A	16	16	□	2" x 2"	
	K	16	4	□	4¼" x 4¼"	⊠
	B	32	16	□	2⅜" x 2⅜"	⧄
Red floral print	M	4	1	□	13¼" x 13¼"	⊠
Light print	Inner border	4	strips	▭	2" x 40"*	
Brown floral print	Outer border	4	Lengthwise strips	▭	6½" x 55"*	
Binding fabric		6	strips	▭	2½" x 40"	

*Strips are cut longer than necessary, and will be trimmed to size later.

Medallion quilts such as this originated in England and were very popular in the late 1700s and early 1800s. Notice how the warm red fabrics advance when surrounded by soft, toned-down colors.

Designed by:
Sharon Evans Yenter

Quilted by:
Sherry D. Rogers

Finished quilt size:
51½" x 51½"

Finished center block size: 12" x 12"

Directions

See *Basic Quiltmaking*, beginning on page 20, for general quiltmaking directions. The instructions here are for making "Diana" exactly as shown. Remember that you can substitute any 6" (finished size) block for the center of the 12" star, and any 3" (finished size) unit will work in the center of the 6" star blocks. Templates for pieces A-L are on pages 15-17.

Block Assembly

All seams ¼". Press seams in direction of arrows unless otherwise instructed.

1. Using 1 of G, 4 of C (beige, tan, or brown prints), 8 of D, and 4 of F, assemble one 12" star block as shown.

2. Using 4 of M, and 8 of J, make 4 flying geese units.

3. Using 96 of A (48 assorted red prints, and 48 assorted beige, tan, and brown prints), and 24 of C (assorted beige, tan, and brown prints), make 12 double-fourpatch blocks.

4. Using 16 of J, make 8 half-square triangle blocks.

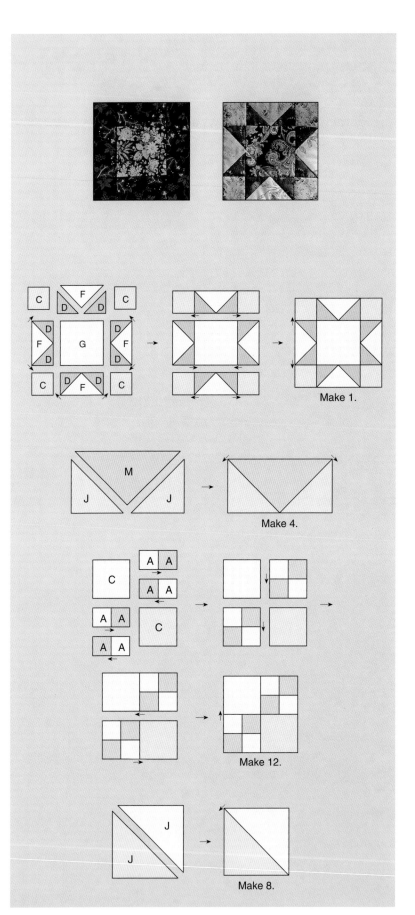

5. Using 4 of C (red prints), 16 of A, 32 of B, and 16 of K, assemble four 6" star blocks.

6. Sew all blocks made in Steps 1-5 together in horizontal rows as shown in the Quilt Assembly Diagram. Press for opposing seams. Join rows together. Press seams in one direction.

Borders

1. Measure length of quilt top through center. Trim 2 of the light print inner border strips to this measurement, and sew to sides of quilt. Press seams toward border.

2. Measure width of quilt top, including borders just added, through center. Trim the remaining 2 light print border strips to this measurement, and sew to top and bottom of quilt. Press seams toward border.

3. Following general instructions in Steps 1 and 2 above, measure, trim, and sew brown floral outer border strips. Add side borders first, then top and bottom borders. Press seams toward outer border.

Finishing

1. Cut the backing fabric into two equal lengths and sew long edges together. Press seam open. Trim backing to 56" x 56".

2. Layer quilt top, batting, and backing. Baste layers together.

3. Plan and mark quilting design as desired.

4. Quilt by hand or machine.

5. Trim the batting and backing even with the quilt top edges.

6. Sew the binding strips together to create one long strip. Bind the quilt edges.

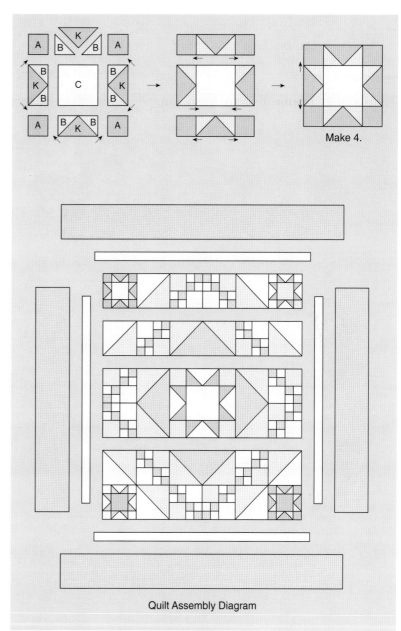

Make 4.

Quilt Assembly Diagram

A scenic print can evoke an era, as shown by this Revolutionary War reproduction fabric. Choose a favorite fabric to create a point of interest in the center of your quilt.

Elizabeth

Materials

Fabric requirements are based on 40" fabric width.

- ⅓ yd. *each* of 9 or more assorted light and medium prints for blocks
- ¼ yd. *each* of 6 or more assorted dark prints for blocks
- ¼ yd. dark stripe for inner border
- 1⅔ yds. dark paisley for outer border
- ⅝ yd. for binding
- 3½ yds. for backing
- 54" x 54" batting

Elizabeth could be considered contemporary but was, in fact, inspired by a Dutch quilt, circa 1800-1825.

Designed by:
Sharon Evans Yenter

Quilted by:
Sherry D. Rogers

Finished quilt size:
50" x 50"

Finished block size:
12" x 12"

Directions

See *Basic Quiltmaking*, beginning on page 20, for general quiltmaking directions. The instructions here are for making "Elizabeth" exactly as shown. You can substitute a square-in-a-square unit for the center of as many blocks as you choose. The square-in-a-square units are made with squares using a simple stitch-and-flip technique. Choose between two cutting methods: numbers for both rotary and template cutting are given on the chart below. Templates are on pages 15-17.

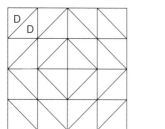 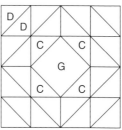

Cutting

Fabric	Piece/ Template	Total Needed	Rotary Cutting Technique			
			# to Cut	Shape	1st Cut	2nd Cut
Assorted light & medium prints	D	172	86	☐	3⅞" x 3⅞"	◩
	G	2	2	☐	6½" x 6½"	
	C	8	8	☐	3½" x 3½"	
Assorted dark prints	D	100	50	☐	3⅞" x 3⅞"	◩
Dark stripe	Inner border	4	strips	▭	1¼" x 40"*	
Dark paisley	Outer border	4 length-wise	strips	▭	6½" x 53"*	
Binding fabric		6	strips	▭	2½" x 40"	

*Strips are cut longer than necessary, and will be trimmed to size later.

Block Assembly

All seams ¼". Press seams in direction of arrows unless otherwise instructed.

Note: *The placement of light, medium, and dark triangles is very important in this quilt. Study the Quilt Assembly Diagram on page 59. Do your planning on a design wall, and don't start sewing until all of your pieces are arranged to your satisfaction. (For square-in-a-square units, fold C squares in half diagonally, wrong sides together. Press lightly. Pin on G squares on your design wall.) You might need to cut a few extra triangles in each value in order to get the look you want.*

1. Using 272 of D, make 136 half-square triangle units as shown.

2. Open up a pressed C square and place it, right sides together, in corner of G square. Sew on pressed line. Trim excess, leaving ¼" seam allowance. Repeat stitch-and-flip technique on opposite diagonal corner, then remaining 2 corners as shown.

3. Using all units made in Steps 1 and 2, assemble 9 blocks.

4. Sew 9 blocks together in horizontal rows as shown in the Quilt Assembly Diagram on page 59. Press for opposing seams. Join rows together. Press seams in one direction.

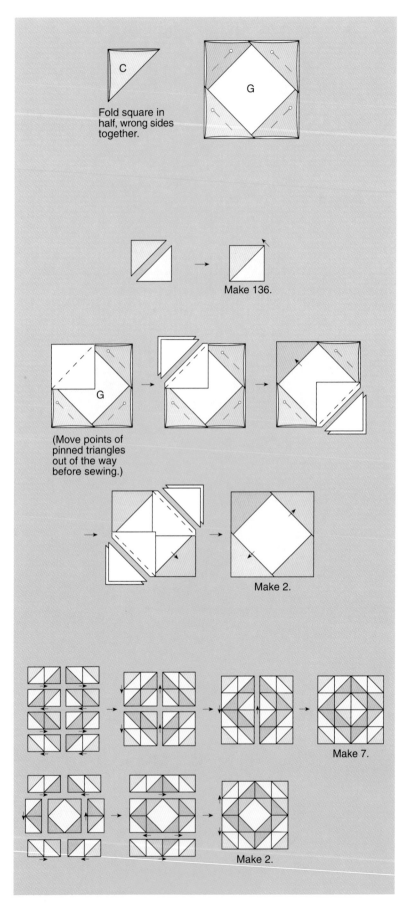

Borders

1. Measure length of quilt top through center. Trim 2 of the dark stripe border strips to this measurement, and sew to sides of quilt. Press seams toward border.
2. Measure width of quilt top, including borders just added, through center. Trim the remaining 2 dark stripe border strips to this measurement, and sew to top and bottom of quilt. Press seams toward border.
3. Following general instructions in Steps 1 and 2 above, measure, trim, and sew dark paisley border strips. Add side borders first, then top and bottom borders. Press seams toward outer border.

Finishing

1. Cut the backing fabric into two equal lengths and sew long edges together. Press seam open. Trim backing to 54" x 54".
2. Layer quilt top, batting, and backing. Baste layers together.
3. Plan and mark quilting design as desired.
4. Quilt by hand or machine.
5. Trim the batting and backing even with the quilt top edges.
6. Sew the binding strips together to create one long strip. Bind the quilt edges.

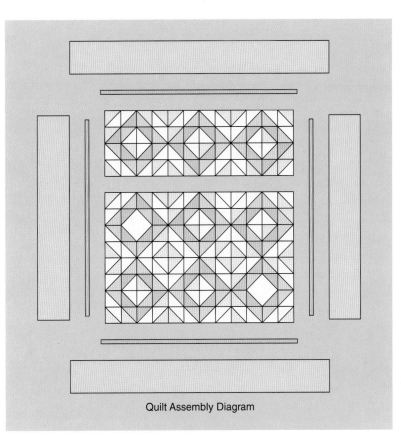

Quilt Assembly Diagram

A large floral peeks out from the center of the block and is defined by surrounding darker fabrics... except for one light print which blends with the center and creates a broken pattern. Study the photo on page 56 and see how this illusion creates areas of lightness and darkness within the quilt.

Fiona

Materials

Fabric requirements are based on 40" fabric width.

- 2½ yds. floral bouquet print for blocks and outer border
- ½ yd. pink toile for blocks
- ¼ yd. green toile for blocks
- ¼ yd. *each* of 7 or more assorted green prints for blocks
- ¼ yd. raspberry tonal print for inner border
- ⅝ yd. for binding
- 3⅜ yds. for backing
- 49" x 55" batting

Directions

See *Basic Quiltmaking*, beginning on page 20, for general quiltmaking directions. The square-in-a-square blocks are made with squares (no triangles!) using a simple stitch-and-flip technique. Choose between two cutting methods: numbers for both rotary and template cutting are given on the chart below. Templates are on pages 15-17.

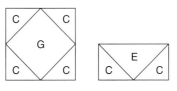

Fiona is a pretty example of large, lush floral prints creating an ambience of graciousness and charm.

Designed by:
Sharon Evans Yenter

Quilted by:
Sherry D. Rogers

Finished quilt size:
44½" x 50½"

Finished block size:
6" x 6"

Cutting

Fabric	Piece/ Template	Total Needed	Rotary Cutting Technique			
			# to Cut	Shape	1st Cut	2nd Cut
Floral bouquet print *(Cut lengthwise strips first)*	Outer border	4 length-wise	strips	▭	6½" x 54"**	
	G	19	19	□	6½" x 6½"	
Pink toile	G	6	6	□	6½" x 6½"	
	E	2	2	▭	3½" x 6½"	
Green toile	G	3	3	□	6½" x 6½"	
	E	2	2	▭	3½" x 6½"	
Assorted green prints	C	120	120	□	3½" x 3½"	
Raspberry tonal print	Inner border	4	strips	▭	1½" x 40"*	
Binding fabric		6	strips	▭	2½" x 40"	

*Strips are cut longer than necessary, and will be trimmed to size later.

**Strips are cut long to allow for selective placement of motifs.

Block Assembly

All seams ¼". Press seams in direction of arrows unless otherwise instructed.

1. Before starting to sew, fold each C square in half diagonally, wrong sides together. Press lightly with iron. Arrange all G and E pieces on your design wall. Pin folded C square to cover corners of G and E pieces as shown. Study the photo on page 60, and the Quilt Assembly Diagram on page 63, and rearrange all of your pieces until you are happy with the overall design.

2. Work with one block at a time. Open up a pressed C square and place it, right sides together, in corner of G square. Sew on pressed line. Trim excess, leaving a ¼" seam allowance. Press seam toward triangle. Repeat stitch-and-flip technique on opposite diagonal corner, then remaining 2 corners as shown.

3. Using same stitch-and-flip technique, sew 2 pressed C squares to each E rectangle.

4. Sew all blocks made in Steps 2 and 3 together in vertical rows as shown in the Quilt Assembly Diagram on page 63. Press seams in one direction. Join rows together. Press seams in one direction.

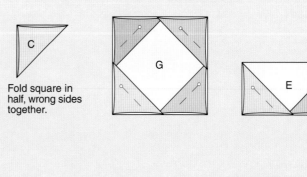

Fold square in half, wrong sides together.

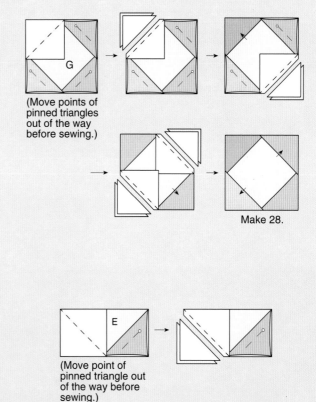

(Move points of pinned triangles out of the way before sewing.)

Make 28.

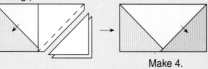

(Move point of pinned triangle out of the way before sewing.)

Make 4.

Borders

1. Measure length of quilt top through center. Trim 2 of the raspberry tonal print border strips to this measurement, and sew to sides of quilt. Press seams toward border.
2. Measure width of quilt top, including borders just added, through center. Trim the remaining 2 raspberry tonal print border strips to this measurement, and sew to top and bottom of quilt. Press seams toward border.
3. Following general instructions in Steps 1 and 2 above, measure, trim, and sew floral bouquet print border strips. Add side borders first, then top and bottom borders. Press seams toward outer border.

Finishing

1. Cut the backing fabric into two equal lengths and sew long edges together. Press seam open. Trim backing to 49" x 55".
2. Layer quilt top, batting, and backing. Baste layers together.
3. Plan and mark quilting design as desired.
4. Quilt by hand or machine.
5. Trim the batting and backing even with the quilt top edges.
6. Sew the binding strips together to create one long strip. Bind the quilt edges.

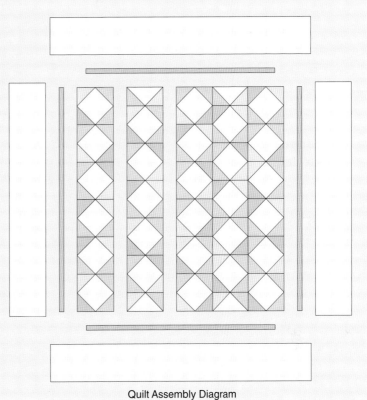

Quilt Assembly Diagram

A multitude of greens, as found in nature, creates a zig-zag line which appears and disappears depending on the fabric values.

Gloria

Materials

Fabric requirements are based on 40" fabric width.

- ⅓ yd. *each* of 6 or more assorted red and beige prints for blocks, side-setting triangles, and corner-setting triangles
- ⅓ yd. *each* of 6 or more assorted green prints for blocks, side-setting triangles, and corner-setting triangles
- ¼ yd. red/green stripe for inner border
- 1⅝ yds. red floral print for outer border
- ⅝ yd. for binding
- 3⅓ yds. for backing
- 52" x 52" batting

Gloria makes a lovely holiday quilt, but would be equally pretty in pastels and florals.

Designed by:
Melissa McCulloch

Quilted by:
Margy Duncan

Finished quilt size:
48" x 48"

Finished block size:
6" x 6"

Directions

See *Basic Quiltmaking*, beginning on page 20, for general quiltmaking directions. Choose between two cutting methods: numbers for both rotary and template cutting are given on the chart below. Templates are on pages 15-17.

*Notice that several "G" blocks make use of scenic designs. Fabrics must be cut "on point" for correct placement. (See Selective Cutting on page 21.)

Cutting

Fabric	Piece/ Template	Total Needed	Rotary Cutting Technique			
			# to Cut	Shape	1st Cut	2nd Cut
Assorted red and beige prints	A	16	16	☐	2" x 2"	
	B	96	48	☐	2⅜" x 2⅜"	◲
	L	16	8	☐	5⅜" x 5⅜"	◲
Assorted green prints	B	96	48	☐	2⅜" x 2⅜"	◲
	L	16	8	☐	5⅜" x 5⅜"	◲
All assorted prints (red, beige, and green)	G*	9	9	☐	6½" x 6½"	
	Side-setting triangles	12	3	☐	9¾" x 9¾"	⊠
	Corner-setting triangles	4	2	☐	5⅛" x 5⅛"	◲
Red/green stripe	Inner border	4	strips	▭	1¼" x 40"**	
Red floral print	Outer border	4 length-wise	strips	▭	6½" x 50"**	
Binding fabric		6	strips	▭	2½" x 40"	

**Strips are cut longer than necessary, and will be trimmed to size later.

Block Assembly

All seams ¼". Press seams in direction of arrows unless otherwise instructed.

1. Using all of A, B, and L pieces, assemble 16 tree blocks as shown.

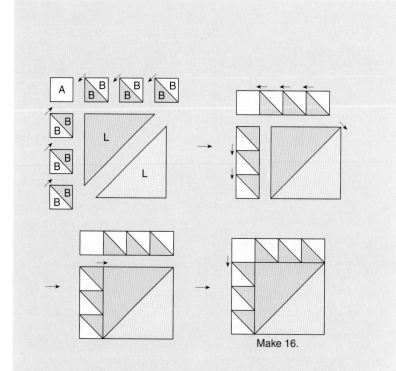

2. Sew 16 tree blocks, 9 of G, 12 side-setting triangles, and 4 corner-setting triangles together in diagonal rows as shown in the Quilt Assembly Diagram on page 67. Press for opposing seams. Join rows together. Press seams in one direction.

Make 16.

Borders

1. Measure length of quilt top through center. Trim 2 of the red/green stripe border strips to this measurement, and sew to sides of quilt. Press seams toward border.

2. Measure width of quilt top, including borders just added, through center. Trim the remaining 2 red/green stripe border strips to this measurement, and sew to top and bottom of quilt. Press seams toward border.

3. Following general instructions in Steps 1 and 2 above, measure, trim, and sew red floral border strips. Add side borders first, then top and bottom borders. Press seams toward outer border.

Notice how the scenic blocks have been cut "on point" to showcase the pretty motifs. This is one time when the grain lines are ignored in cutting. Be careful when you stitch the seams as they will be on the bias and will tend to stretch. See page 21 for selective cutting instructions.

Finishing

1. Cut the backing fabric into two equal lengths and sew long edges together. Press seam open. Trim backing to 52" x 52".
2. Layer quilt top, batting, and backing. Baste layers together.
3. Plan and mark quilting design as desired.
4. Quilt by hand or machine.
5. Trim the batting and backing even with the quilt top edges.
6. Sew the binding strips together to create one long strip. Bind the quilt edges.

Decorating Tip

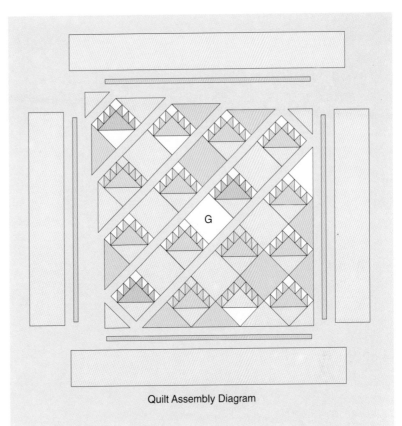

Quilt Assembly Diagram

A miniature tree with small ornaments complements the size of the motifs, such as the church and skaters, inside the quilt. Surround your wall hanging with familiar family collectibles and photos.

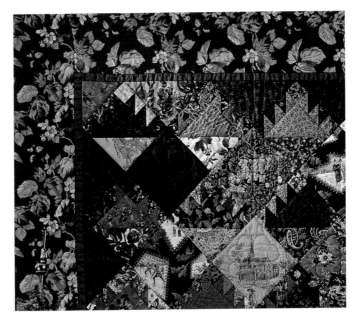

Do you see how the high and low contrast invites you to study this quilt so you can identify the trees? Now you see them. Now you don't!

Heather

Materials

Fabric requirements are based on 40" fabric width.

- ⅓ yd. *each* of 12 or more assorted pink, green, and beige prints for blocks, side-setting triangles, and corner-setting triangles
  (Include 1 or 2 toiles, and at least 1 large floral in your fabric assortment. If you use only 1 large floral, purchase ⅔ yd. for selective cutting of bouquets.)

- ¼ yd. pink floral print for inner border
- 2⅜ yds. green toile for outer border and binding
- 3⅞ yds. for backing
- 61" x 61" batting

Small tone-on-tones from your stash, mixed with toiles and a large floral bouquet, create a charming combination as shown in this pretty quilt.

Designed by:
Sharon Evans Yenter

Quilted by:
Sherry D. Rogers

Finished quilt size:
56½" x 56½"

Finished block size:
6" x 6"

Directions

See *Basic Quiltmaking*, beginning on page 20, for general quiltmaking directions. The instructions here are for making "Heather" exactly as shown. Notice that the blocks have either a fourpatch or onepatch unit at their centers. You can use more or fewer fourpatches as desired, or substitute another 3" (finished size) unit for the block centers. Choose between two cutting methods: numbers for both rotary and template cutting are given on the chart below. Templates are on pages 15-17.

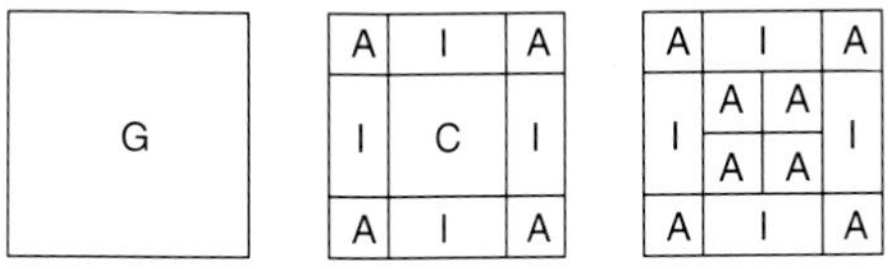

*Notice that several "G" blocks make use of large florals and toiles. Pictorial fabrics must be cut "on point" for correct placement. (See Selective Cutting on page 21.)

Cutting

Fabric	Piece/ Template	Total Needed	Rotary Cutting Technique			
			# to Cut	Shape	1st Cut	2nd Cut
Assorted pink, green, and beige prints	G*	16	16	☐	6½" x 6½"	
	C	14	14	☐	3½" x 3½"	
	A	144	144	☐	2" x 2"	
	I	100	100	▭	2" x 3½"	
	Side-setting triangles	16	4	☐	9¾" x 9¾"	⊠
	Corner-setting triangles	4	2	☐	5⅛" x 5⅛"	◺
Pink floral print	Inner border	5	strips	▭	1¼" x 40"	
Green toile (Cut lengthwise strips first)	Outer border	4 lengthwise	strips	▭	6½" x 59"**	
	Binding	7	strips	▭	2½" x 40"	

**Strips are cut longer than necessary, and will be trimmed to size later.

Block Assembly

All seams ¼". Press seams in direction of arrows unless otherwise instructed.

1. Using 14 of C, 56 of A, and 56 of I, assemble 14 blocks as shown.

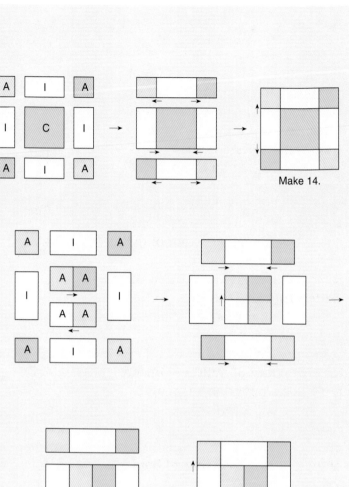

Make 14.

2. Using 88 of A, and 44 of I, assemble 11 blocks as shown.

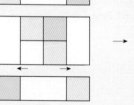
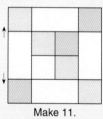

3. Sew 16 of G, all blocks made in Steps 1 and 2, 16 side-setting triangles, and 4 corner-setting triangles together in diagonal rows as shown in the Quilt Assembly Diagram on page 71. Press for opposing seams. Join rows together. Press seams in one direction.

Make 11.

Borders

1. Sew 5 pink floral border strips together, end-to-end, to make one long strip. Measure length of quilt top through center. From the long strip, cut 2 strips to this measurement, and sew to sides of quilt. Press seams toward border.

2. Measure width of quilt top, including borders just added, through center. Cut 2 pink floral strips (from the long strip) to this measurement, and sew to top and bottom of quilt. Press seams toward border.

3. Measure length of quilt top through center. Trim 2 of the green toile border strips to this measurement, and sew to sides of quilt. Press seams toward border.

4. Measure width of quilt top, including borders just added, through center. Trim the remaining 2 green toile border strips to this measurement, and sew to top and bottom of quilt. Press seams toward border.

Finishing

1. Cut the backing fabric into two equal lengths and sew long edges together. Press seam open. Trim backing to 61" x 61".

2. Layer quilt top, batting, and backing. Baste layers together.

3. Plan and mark quilting design as desired.

4. Quilt by hand or machine.

5. Trim the batting and backing even with the quilt top edges.

6. Sew the binding strips together to create one long strip. Bind the quilt edges.

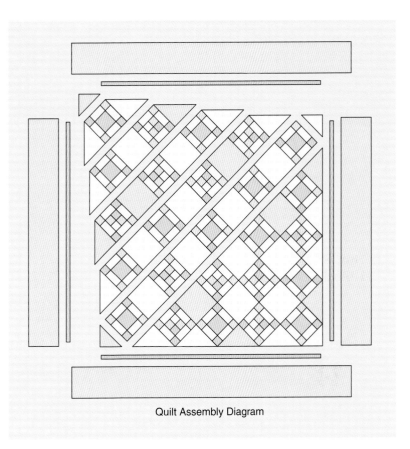

Quilt Assembly Diagram

Notice the combinations of pink, coral-pink, blue-pink, and deep red in this piece and in the flowers on the opposite page. Analagous colors can make a quilt, or a bouquet, sparkle.

Credits

EDITOR: Wendy Slotboom

TECHNICAL EDITOR: Laurie Shifrin

PHOTOGRAPHY: Melanie Blair

PHOTO STYLING: Sharon Evans Yenter
and Melissa McCulloch

ART DIRECTION AND DESIGN: Barbara Schmitt

ILLUSTRATIONS: Wendy Slotboom and Brian Metz

Published by In The Beginning, Inc.

Acknowledgments

Thanks to all the wonderful people involved in this and past projects. I am truly blessed to work with such talented people. I keep writing books to expose quiltmakers to the joys of creativity, but also because our team makes it so much fun and a continuous learning experience for me.

Editor Wendy Slotboom is hardworking and precise. Her enthusiasm for her job is contagious. Although her cat, Toby, does not appear in this book, we know you'll see him again!

Designer Barbara Schmitt is inventive and thoughtful. She always has just the right idea to make a book special.

Photographer Melanie Blair added exceptional color and ambiance to her photos. Her professional care and attention to every detail is amazing.

Special thanks to Melissa McCulloch for her lovely quilts and sense of style and color.

Quilters Margy Duncan, Paula Prominski, and Sherry D. Rogers made our quilts "come to life" with dimension and beauty.

Sharon Evans Yenter pictured with company mascot and grandson, Zachary.

Author

Sharon is the owner of In The Beginning Fabrics in Seattle, Washington. She is the author of *Floral Bouquet Quilts*, and co-author with Marsha McCloskey of *Blended Quilts from In The Beginning*. Her goal for the past 27 years has been to educate men and women about the importance of quilt-making as a historical, artistic, and social experience. Her store is a mecca for locals and visitors to the Seattle area.

Resources

Fabric collections and books by Sharon Evans Yenter; and fabrics, books, and Precision Trimmers™ by Marsha McCloskey are available at your local quilt shop or you may inquire at:

In The Beginning Fabrics
8201 Lake City Way NE
Seattle, WA 98115
206.523.8862
www.inthebeginningfabrics.com

Quilt Wall® is available at your local quilt shop or you may order from:

Keepsake Quilting
PO Box 1618
Center Harbor, NH 03226-1618
1.800.865.9458